WHY WE BEHAVE

Why We Behave

A Practical Guide

By Maurice Cayem, PhD, MSPP

To order additional copies of this book, contact:
Xlibris Corporation
1-888-795-4274
www.Xlibris.com
Orders@Xlibris.com

59384

CONTENTS

DEDICATION

First and foremost, I would like to thank and honor my mother for financing this project and believing in me. My thanks also goes out to my wife and kids for giving me much more than money in the form of support and encouragement.

Particular thanks goes to my son Daniel R. Cayem for assisting me in the research for this work and for compiling the bibliography. He has been a valuable assistant throughout this project.

And lastly, I would like to thank all the developmentally disabled people I serve, for teaching me much of what I have written.

CHAPTER 1

An Introduction

I started out attempting to write a book on applied behavior analysis, which is the science and practice I have been engaged in for more than thirty years. However, as I got deeper in the discussion and research on the subject, I realized that much of the concepts and approaches I had been using would not actually qualify as belonging to the field of applied behavior analysis. I must confess that in the early seventies, I took great interest in a new science called *sociobiology* that was developing at the time. And in my laboratory experiments, I dealt with animals, fish in particular, and was deep into comparative psychology and physiological psychology. These fields had a significant impact on my view of behaviorism and the practice of applied behavior analysis in later years. However, when dealing with extreme behaviors, I discovered that oftentimes the problems we were dealing with and the behaviors we were observing and attempting to change had no environmental antecedents other than some biological disturbance that occurred early in the developmental process, and usually before birth, such as genetic anomalies, birth trauma, and many unknown conditions. Many of my patients were on medications, which, no doubt, had a significant impact on their behaviors. I eventually went back to school and earned a master of science degree in psychopharmacology to better understand this dynamic of having medication interfere with mood and level of agitation and arousal. These influences had shaped my understanding and practice of applied behavior analysis, and I really did not realize that what I was practicing was not purely a behavioral approach. This realization came as I began writing this book. Up until that time, I had viewed myself as a behavioral psychologist and have been practicing behavior therapy for my entire career.

As I began to put my views to paper, I quickly realized how much of what I taught to the staff that took care of my developmentally disabled patients was *not* applied behavior analysis. But whatever the influences that I used were, they were all put to use to change behaviors within the applied behavior analysis approach. I found that what I had been using was an approach that I characterize as *behavioral sociobiology*. So to be fair, I must warn you that this is *not* a traditional approach or view of applied behavior analysis, although that is what my practice provides. The fact that I bring to the practice influences outside that science does not, in my view, negate the fact that I am a practicing behaviorist. On the contrary, I feel that this provides me with a deeper and more complete picture of the person I am attempting to serve.

My general view of anything consists of an onion approach of understanding that which I am attempting to understand. By this I mean that once I see something, such as a person biting themselves or banging their head, I understand that this is only the outer layer of the onion. Underneath that layer, there is another layer—let's say the biological layer—then another, maybe the social layer; then another, the familial layer, etc., until we are dealing with the biochemical layer, not to mention nutrition, level of stimulation, or exposure to the world as well as other influences. In a way, this onion approach assumes that all of these layers are part of one integrated organism, so that a disturbance in any layer can affect the behavior of all the layers of the onion.

Things are not as simple as they appear, nor are they as complex as they seem. I have had cases where a slew of bizarre behaviors were eliminated simply by stabilizing someone's sleep pattern or nutrition. In the late seventies and early eighties, megavitamin therapy was common for autistic children, just as fat diets and hormone therapy for seizures. Most approaches work for some but not all individuals. What works depends on the individual's constitution at birth. Behavioral problems are not as simple as specific infections that can be treated with an antibiotic, or a broken leg that can be set and placed in a cast until it heals. Behaviors are dynamic adjustment reactions to our environments. Thus, we have to closely observe the interaction between external as well as internal events that are impacting the person we are trying to help. My approach is not necessarily to dissect the individual on every level or layer of the onion paradigm, but, rather, start with the simplest and most common causes of behavioral problems, which is the immediate environment. But if that is not effective in eliminating or significantly reducing the inappropriate behavior, then you must go deeper and deeper until a solution is found. Unfortunately, a solution is sometimes never found, but what is achieved is an improved adjustment to one's environment.

Behaviors are the expressions of our needs. They are the language of our being. It should come as no surprise to anyone to hear that we often don't know why we behave. But the body knows why it behaves in this manner. And if only we could be more in tune with our bodies, we would know why we behave. However, if even an intact and healthy individual does not know why they behave, can you imagine how baffled a developmentally disabled person must feel concerning their behaviors?

Although most of my work and experience has been with the developmentally disabled population, I have attempted to answer the question as to why we behave in general. There are, of course, differences between intact organisms and developmentally disabled individuals, but the differences are only those of degree and ability to control and understand and not differences in how things work. The mechanisms of behavior are the same for all of us. This includes all organisms on the planet and not just human beings. There are lawful relationships between ourselves and our interaction with the world or environment. And it is these relationships that I will be focusing on. Thus, this book is not restricted to the developmentally disabled population. Nor is it restricted by the concepts and parameters of applied behavior analysis. It is simply my answer to the question of why we behave after over thirty years of studying the subject.

What I have tried to provide for the reader is not a textbook account of behavior. You can get that in many very good publications on the topic. In this book, I have attempted to walk the reader through an experiential model of behavior that I have not found anywhere else in the literature. Parts of what I am discussing can be found in separate publications, but the complete picture and view of behaviors that I am about to describe comes completely from my experience in the field of behavior therapy and the concepts and ideas I have turned to in my efforts to help and understand those whom I aim to help.

Since my laboratory experiments in the early seventies, I have not engaged in any scientific research. Thus, the concepts and ideas that I present are those that I have used and developed while engaging in the practice of behavior therapy, and I am in no way attempting to present "evidence" that I have discovered in research. Again, I am aiming for and attempting to provide an experiential model of behavior and to focus much on how our experience of the world affects us and our behaviors in it.

Brief Outline of Chapters

In chapter 2, I discuss some background information and introduce you to sociobiology and its implications. I then discuss worldviews in chapter 3 and some historical basis to what I am about to explain. In the fourth chapter, I begin to explain my theory of behaviors. In chapter 5, I describe what behaviors are, followed by a discussion on the functional analysis in chapter 6, where I introduce the parameter of emotions, which are usually not part of the traditional behavioral approach. In chapter 7, I focus on emotions themselves and how they relate to behaviors. Then in chapter 8, I talk about the influences that determine behaviors. Starting in chapter 9, I begin looking at how we can achieve behavioral change and the precursors of intervention. In chapter 10, I briefly describe the actual intervention and how it should be structured. Chapter 11 talks about the target population that is the most common recipient of behavior therapy. Chapter 12 attempts to sensitize the reader to those subject to behavior therapy. Then in chapter 13, I talk about the mind-set, or global intervention approach, followed by a chapter on science and religion. The reason for this is that it has become an issue for some, and I attempt to present a practical approach to how these two can work together without attempting to promote one or the other. I then try to summarize what all of this may mean to you, the reader, and how this information can be of use to you in your own life. We all have to behave, and no one is exempt from that.

Thus, the more we know about what influences our behavior, the more we are able to control it.

The chapters are self-contained and can be read separately, but for you to understand what I am trying to accomplish for the reader, the book should be read from beginning to end since it represents a progression of ideas that fit together.

CHAPTER 2

Background

When I was a young lad, it was obvious to all in the family that I was different. The third child in a family of three children, I was more active than the other two. I was hyperactive. And as Joe Namath once said, "Till I was thirteen, I thought my name was Shut Up." Growing up in such an environment, I got the feeling that something was wrong with me. And with the constant intervention at home and school due to my behavioral issues, the environment I was in became oppressive. At fifteen, I had had enough and left home to live on the streets. I start with this little piece of behavior because I want to set what I hope to be the tone of the entire book—that in the face of losing shelter, food, and an otherwise nurturing environment, or being free from the constant oppressive *feeling* that I didn't belong, I chose the latter and not the former. The prime motivating factor was the feeling that I could do whatever I wanted to and was forever free from the oppression, which I found stifling. I must mention that the environment then was much safer than it is today. Nevertheless, I still had to find food and a place to sleep at night, and survive with no prospect of a job. However, those things were secondary to the freedom that I felt when I was totally on my own with no one to answer to. And it is that feeling that drove me to where I am today.

Why we do the things we do has been a long-standing preoccupation of the human race. Many prophets, philosophers, and scientists have spent lifetimes attempting to learn and describe what causes behavior. In the following pages, I will suggest a view of human behavior that rests on a unique way of interpreting the current facts. I am not here attempting to prove anything in this work. One can prove just about anything using selective pieces of information that support their particular viewpoint. However, on closer scrutiny of the material, one can always take apart an interpretation of the facts and come up with a different conclusion. Thus, my aim is not to offer proof but, rather, a point of view for the reader to consider the theoretical structure put forth based on his or her own experience of the world. I will, when appropriate, mention certain studies and scientific facts that support my theory. However, the aim is not to present a scientific doctrine of behavior. Rather, I want to focus on the internal variables usually ignored by behaviorists when discussing behaviorism and offer a practical guide as to how to interpret, analyze, and intervene with behaviors in the field using these internal variables. My belief is that these factors also control behaviors, just as the objective variables that predominate all of the current research on behaviorism. In fact, I am sure many behaviorists will disagree with my conclusions since they violate the vehement and stringent insistence on *not* paying attention to those internal, nonmeasurable variables when discussing behaviorism and the causation of behavior. In behaviorism, only observable and measurable factors in the environment are to be used to explain, change, and evaluate the effectiveness of behavioral plans. I disagree with this view on many levels, but primarily because it is an incomplete picture of the human experience. I have been a practicing behavioral psychologist for over twenty years, and experience has taught me that while behaviorism is the best form of therapy to practice with individuals exhibiting behavioral problems, what is behind the behavioral problems is usually a feeling or emotion that is driving those behaviors. Yet behaviorism usually ignores those variables and insists on focusing only on observable events. This one point has been the primary inspiration for the current work. I believe in behaviorism, but that doesn't exclude other streams of knowledge and experience relative to behavior as being irrelevant or unusable variables in the field of changing behavior. The practice of applied behavior analysis does not require the exclusion of all other sources of information one may have at their disposal. If we are in the business of changing behavior for the better, then we do everything possible to bring about that change. Whether it is a hunch, a certain feeling, or an undefined relationship, this emotional experience still moves us. It makes us behave.

Since the late 1930s to the present, behaviorism has been the science that focuses exclusively on behaviors, the factors affecting it, and the variables controlling it. That field has been labeled as behaviorism, then respondent and operant conditioning, then behavior modification, and currently it has come to be referred to as applied behavior analysis. In the field of applied behavior analysis, or behaviorism in general, the scientist remains focused on environmental variables exclusively, because it is these variables that we can see, describe objectively, and manipulate which can be shown to be responsible for how people behave. This relationship between behavior and environmental variables can be shown to control behavior by simply changing the parameters of those variables and observing the resulting change in behavior.

B. F. Skinner, probably the best-known behavioral psychologist, spent much time in explaining and attempting to convince psychologists that emotions, or what he called "private events," have no place in a science of behavior because these variables cannot be measured, manipulated, or controlled. Thus, it was of no use to utilize them in any scientific way. Up until that time (1938), most psychological work was focused almost exclusively on those private events. The field of psychology was dominated by psychoanalysis, free association, and the description of mental events. Hence Skinner's need to shift the focus and provide a counterbalance to the prevailing views in an attempt to objectify psychology and bring it in line with the empirical tradition of the other sciences. However, the result for behaviorism has been somewhat of a "throw the baby out with the bathwater" approach to these so-called private events. Thus, behaviorists do not concern themselves with emotions, drives, or feelings. They focus exclusively on environmental variables that can be altered and controlled to control behavior. But I would argue that just because we cannot see and measure such events is no reason to disregard them altogether. Even Skinner could not completely disregard them. This is why he devoted so many pages and chapters to this subject but still concluding their inappropriateness for a science of behavior. I counted 154 incidents of referring to emotions in his book *Verbal Behavior*. It could be argued, however, that we can indeed manipulate such internal private events. Most advertising, political speech, sales pitches, and other forms of manipulation are geared toward doing just that.

In the pages that follow, I will make the case that not only do we need to pay attention and focus on these internal experiences, but that through the examples—such as advertising, politics, sales, as well as my own experiences in the field practicing behavior intervention with real people—I hope to demonstrate that these aspects of behavior, these private events, or, more simply, emotions, are sometimes much more powerful than the manipulation of known objective variables. Emotions are prime movers in the causation of behaviors.

Let me be very clear that the intention here is not to *detract* anything from behaviorism as it stands but, rather, to *add* another dimension that can be of use in the control of human behavior when applied in real-world situations. Indeed, this was Skinner's primary concern, as it has been my own. However, I am attempting to extend that vision of a behaviorism that is more inclusive of variables that cannot be seen but can often be used and manipulated to achieve a behavioral change in the individuals we work with.

The first point to be made concerning these private events or emotions and their suitability for a science of human behavior is that applied behavior analysis, while it is based on the scientific principles of behavior analysis, is not itself a science when applied in the real world but, rather, the application of scientific principles in the natural environment to offer practical solutions to socially problematic behaviors. Thus, although I agree that private events cannot be measured and it would be difficult to experimentally manipulate such variables, I have found that in practice, taking into account biological and emotional factors, which are primarily private events, can be of significant use in the practical control of behavior. Having had most of my behavioral experience with a population that is significantly impacted biologically—the developmentally disabled population—I have been forced to take those disabilities into account in analyzing, designing, and implementing behavioral plans and have found that some variables, although they remain seemingly inaccessible to manipulation by the interventionist, are, nevertheless quite useful in diagnosing behavioral problems and picking out a course of action that can prevent serious outbursts, if taken into account. The general model or orientation that I have come to consider is that of a *behavioral sociobiology*, which I will describe shortly.

The second point to be made is that just because we cannot see, measure, and quantify a variable does not mean that we cannot use and manipulate that variable to our own advantage. Or if we cannot access it to manipulate it, we can at least use that information in the formulation of our plan of action. For example, let us say we had to deal with someone that is suffering from loneliness, abandonment, or rejection when first placed in a long-term residential facility. It is difficult, if not impossible, to determine the exact emotion and how intense it is, or how long it will last, etc.; but whatever it is, it does have an impact on behavior and has behavioral symptoms that we can see and measure. These may include listlessness, withdrawal, lack of appetite, resistiveness, and the list goes on. Appropriate diagnosis of the problem would obviously be useful in the treatment process. Behaviorally, doing a functional analysis (see section below on the functional analysis) would indicate that the lack of the ability to go into her own room, be with her family, and do the things she used to do, such as sit in her favorite chair, are all no longer possible. The new environment is not familiar and produces some anxiety in her, which is a private or emotional event usually not considered in the functional analysis since it is not behavioral. But anxiety can be observed behaviorally by how much more cautious she is in responding to people, how well she accepts touch, how much fidgeting she engages in with her hands.

An appropriate replacement behavior may be to have a surrogate mother, but often, this is not possible since this is something that has to naturally occur. We could attempt to increase her involvement with her parents, but this is not always possible since we are not able to control her parents' behavior. So we resort to appeasing her by allowing her not to participate since this provokes resistance. However, leaving her alone too much will simply reinforce her withdrawal and not help her incorporate into the group. Walking this fine line between leaving her alone and encouraging her to participate must be implemented carefully to achieve the desired result. What we want to do is make her feel at home. Behaviorally, we will be introducing all of the elements that she was used to, such as bringing in her favorite chair from home, watching her favorite shows on TV, and listening to her favorite music. But the real results never come from these superficial measures. The real turnaround moment is when she emotionally bonds with a staff member that truly likes her and she reciprocates that emotion. While we did not directly manipulate a variable that is invisible and has no identifiable parameters, the problem was resolved by affecting that variable emotionally. Thus the need and value of taking into account internal states that cannot be measured or seen but do result in behavioral change, which is the main point of intervention. Thus, if we cannot force this to happen, we can facilitate this process by assigning different staff to her until one bonds with her.

In the following chapters, I will discuss and suggest possible standard ways of how to incorporate those internal variables into a functional analysis, and later into a behavioral plan. But for now, I am simply pointing out the need for a *behavioral sociobiology*. What I am describing is a behavioral approach that takes into account the biological basis of behavior as well as the social context in which it occurs. That social setting, or environment, has a significant impact on behavior through the development of relationships with others. Biological entities undergo chemical reactions and imbalances in the body that are experienced as emotions. Those can be measured and manipulated, but not simply by observation. It is suggested that these biological changes, which cannot be directly observed, are responsible for the motivation of behavior.

The third and final point I would like to make before going into the discussion on sociobiology is that we have to keep our goal in mind. The entire purpose for a science of behavior is to achieve the practical control of behaviors so that we can build and develop those behaviors that are most advantageous to the specie while reducing those that are least advantageous. If that is the goal, which is what Skinner and others have espoused, then any avenue of knowledge that we can use that achieves this purpose should be welcome. To attempt to reduce all human experience in behavioral and tangible terms is like the physicist studying only those things he or she can see. In reality, much of what is studied in even such a concrete science as physics is not what is actually seen, such as subatomic particles, but the behaviors of those particles.

The existence of those particles is presumed based on behavioral traces. I see no difference between that and the study of human behavior. We can indeed use emotions and emotional states as part of a functional analysis because we can observe their behavioral consequences once those parameters have been manipulated.

The behavioral consequences alone cannot account for the intensity or depth of those emotional experiences; they are inferred from long-range observation of behaviors such as inferring the convictions of Mother Teresa from watching her years of dedication to her work. If you were to watch any of her behaviors in the moment it occurs, you could not see or know or establish the strength of her behaviors. But after years of behaving a certain way, one can infer some kind of guiding emotional fulfillment that is reinforcing to her that goes far beyond any reinforcement documented in the three-dimensional world we live in, such as monetary rewards, physical comforts, and such. I would argue that we actually do not live in that world alone. That world that we can see and touch is simply the aspect of existence that is coarse enough to be observed by the naked eye. Much of what exists in nature cannot be seen without the help of instruments that go far beyond our own capabilities. We simply have not advanced scientifically to the point where we can see and measure emotions, although we are well on the way of doing so, with machines, not through direct observation.

One interesting experiment done on emotions suggests that emotions can be influenced and perceived by the context in which they occur. And the interpretation of the emotion can indeed be manipulated. Schachter and Singer in 1962 designed an experiment whereby the subjects were administered shots of epinephrine and misinformed about its effect. Epinephrine is a hormone produced by the adrenal gland that enables the body to meet conditions of stress. Taken by itself, it produces an increased heart rate and shakiness, much as if someone was excited or emotionally aroused about something. Subjects were told that they were being injected with a new vitamin compound suproxin and that they are to wait in a room with actors that were either acting euphoric or angry for a few minutes to study the effect it had on them. The subjects that waited with the euphoric actor reported that the drug made them feel happy and euphoric while the ones that spent time with the angry actor reported that the drug made them feel angry.

The experimenters were advancing the theory that emotions are interpreted based on context. But I wish to point out that first, emotions can be manipulated, and this occurs frequently in normal human interactions. In this case, through injection of a chemical substance leading to physiological arousal, and performance by an actor that provided the context for the interpretation of that internal state (Psychwiki.com, The Schachter-Singer Theory of Emotion, 1962). But more importantly, I wish to point out that emotions are the product of biochemical changes in the physiology of the organism, and their expression and experience can be manipulated by the environments in which they occur. I will discuss this aspect of emotions more fully later, but it should be kept in mind that although emotions cannot be directly observed, their behavioral symptoms and emotions can actually be measured with instruments. The lie detector test, or Galvanic Skin Response (GSR), uses these physiological changes to infer whether the individual is telling the truth or not. Thus, these internal events we call emotions are very real events that impact behavior and should not be ignored.

The Need for a Behavioral Sociobiology

Sociobiology is a science that was first developed by Edward O. Wilson, professor of zoology and curator in entomology at the Museum of Comparative Zoology at Harvard University in the early 1970s, and the science has since evolved into what is now called *evolutionary psychology*, although I still prefer the term *sociobiology* to designate that we are biological organisms operating in a social environment. There have been many arguments against sociobiology from behavioral purists implying that the two views are not compatible or that we don't have to resort to biological causation that cannot be observed since we can account for behavior strictly using observable environmental parameters. I will attempt to blur that line. This seeming incompatibility of the two sciences is as artificial as the incompatibility of science and religion, and frankly, we need to evolve beyond such dualistic ideas. One can argue that these are simply different ends of the same spectrum. Both seek the truth, but one demands physical and tangible proof, and the other requires faith only. Again, I will attempt to blur that line as well. Sociobiology is simply the systematic study of the biological basis of all social behavior. Biological beings are saddled with certain requirements to maintain the health of the system, and our social structure determines how those requirements will be met. In other words, our behavior will be determined by the social structure or environment we find ourselves in to meet our various biological requirements to survive. Thus, there is no competition between behaviorism, which deals with individual behaviors, and sociobiology, which deals with internal triggers that provoke behaviors within a social setting. Discoveries in either science will contribute to our understanding of behavior. Biological entities seem predisposed to seek an understanding of how they maintain themselves and propagate themselves on the planet. The development of sociobiology was an attempt to unify many sciences and put them all under one umbrella—including genetics, biology, population biology, physiology, ethology, sociology, psychology, and comparative psychology, to name a few. In short, it includes any science that has anything to say about social behavior. In fact, according to Wilson (1975) "sociobiology is defined as the systematic study of the biological basis of all social behavior" (Wilson, 1975).

Important parameters affecting the emission of behaviors in sociobiology consist of several constraints on each specie depending on their particular structure and constitution. The most salient constraints consist of the following:

- genetic constraints
- biological constraints
- behavioral constraints
- group structure
- cooperative tendencies

Thus, for sociobiology, it is these variables among many others that affect and provoke behavior, most of which cannot themselves be controlled.

Genetic Constraints

One of the strongest arguments that one can make in reference to how internal events that are unseen can be responsible for behaviors is the observation that within the nature of all animals, the motivation to survive and procreate is omnipresent. There is no animal known that will not attempt to escape from danger or from events that could be harmful to them. And all animals, if given the opportunity, will copulate to procreate. We can do little about these behavioral tendencies, which are also constraints on behavior. The only factor affecting the evolution of the genetic structure is reproducing offspring that will in turn reproduce themselves and, if their traits favor their survivability and reproductive potential, will help the specie evolve in that direction. From the evolutionary standpoint of sociobiology, all behaviors are, in effect, techniques to reproduce the gene. That gene is encased in every member of the specie who is the temporary carrier of that gene material and whose main purpose is to protect that gene material until it is reproduced as many times as possible to increase the chance for survival of its specie. This behavioral propensity is not a learned behavior. It appears to be inherent in all biological entities studied thus far. Again, although this drive or need cannot be directly observed, the goal-oriented behavior of the organism can be observed; and thus, the underlying drive or need is inferred. The environment has little to do with bringing about this tendency to behave in a sexual or protective manner. The only thing that can happen in reference to the environment is that it can interfere with or facilitate the organism's ability to express its behavioral tendency by either providing the opportunity to engage in the behavior or not. Those organisms that do not express these tendencies, due to trauma or damage to the organism, renders them nonfunctional, and they are labeled as developmentally disabled. In the natural world, most of these nonfunctional members of the specie are tolerated but are also left to fend for themselves or perish. Assuming an intact organism, we can see and observe behaviors that will consistently protect the individual and attempt to reproduce itself through sexual contact with a member of the opposite sex within that specie. Thus, the primary motivation of all behavior consists of this internal and inferred tendency that cannot be directly observed or measured. But these aspects of our genetic structure that are elusive to us, at least in reference to the objective and scientific measure of their existence, do not deny their existence.

The fact that we can do little about our genetic structure, coupled with the inability to directly observe its presence, taking genetic predispositions into account can be of great help to us in reference to shaping behavior more effectively. For example, if someone is genetically predisposed to be a visual learner, we can structure a behavioral plan that relies more on visual demonstration, such as using calendars to track progress to a goal for visual feedback rather than using auditory instructions or reading material (see Learning Modality Assessment in the appendix). Genetic variables, although they cannot be directly manipulated, can be used to help design a more effective behavior intervention plan by keeping these constraints in mind. Going along with someone's own tendencies is a well-known martial arts technique of pushing the individual in the direction in which they were already heading. This is much more effective than blocking them and getting hurt in the process. Designing behavior plans or lesson plans to teach someone anything can be achieved more easily and effectively if you are working with someone's strengths rather than focusing on their weaknesses. The weaknesses can be slowly introduced from a place of strength and familiarity. For example, when I had to teach language-impaired hyperactive children about colors, I knew they loved rhymes like those in children's books. I suppose that's why they are there. So I made up short rhymes about each color with an illustration that was entirely out of the color it represents. Thus, I would have a depiction of a "brown town," "green bean," etc., so that once they make the association of the item with the color, they can generalize the color to other objects and thus learn their colors.

Biological Constraints

Biological constraints can, to some degree, be altered with training, exercise, and exposure to certain stimuli, but still, only within a narrow range. One comes to the world with certain attributes that favor certain endeavors. This does not mean that those favorable attributes will have a chance to flourish; this will depend on environmental opportunities. However, one also comes to the world with certain deficits such as breathing problems or the propensity for infections that result in getting sick more often, etc., making certain vocational aspirations almost impossible to pursue. We have all heard of exceptions to these rules, but that is just what they are, exceptions. I am not here to account for every exception ever encountered. Suffice it to say that I will cling to generalities throughout this book. I am interested in the general nature of our world, which is what we must all be concerned about within any social structure. Biological constraints place limits on what behaviors can be engaged in. There is a concept often used in sociobiology called *specie specific behaviors*. These behaviors are engaged in by the entire specie but not engaged in by other species. For example, birds can fly, and we cannot. Fish can breathe underwater, and we cannot. Thus, the range of behaviors possible for any particular specie is limited by their physiological and biological structure.

In reference to a behavioral sociobiology, the belief is that it is our biology that triggers behaviors through chemical imbalances that are experienced as emotions. These *emotions*, due to their ability to make the organism uncomfortable, can be transformed into *motivations* to act or behave. And the direction of all behavior is toward reducing the discomfort. Thus, the primary motivating factor in all behavior, or the function of all behaviors, are, in one way or another, ways to soothe one's own emotional state and satisfy one's own requirements of the moment, one's own anxiety level or contentment level.

Behavioral Constraints

Behaviors are actions taken on and applied to the environment that surrounds the organism and are limited in scope by the type of environment the organism finds themselves in. For example, if the individual is born in an inland environment, miles away from any beach, they will not have the opportunity to develop behaviors that require the ocean, such as surfing or deep-sea fishing. But they may become quite skilled horseback riders. Those born in the jungle may know how to easily survive in that environment and travel by swinging on trees; others of the same specie will have a much harder time adapting, depending on how different their native environment is to the one they find themselves in. The most significant aspect of behavioral constraints is the addictive nature of behavior. Almost everything we do becomes a routine, a program, a set of responses weaved together so closely that they seem to be one script that can be implemented without even thinking.

Behavioral constraints can be modified with the use of applied behavior analysis techniques, but as we all know, these require the control of variables that the behaviors we are attempting to affect are a function of. Sometimes, this aspect of behaviorism is impossible to achieve in the natural world. Anyone who has attempted to shape a child's behavior with the help of family members bent on reinforcing inappropriate behaviors because they know the child better than the interventionist can appreciate the difficulty of achieving behavioral change while trying to control such spoiler variables. We simply cannot control the environment in the natural world to the same degree that we can in the laboratory. This is not to say that applied behavior analysis cannot overcome some of these obstacles. In fact, this is what is very powerful about applied behavior analysis—the ability to achieve change, even in the midst of many variables that cannot be controlled. So long as you can control one or two main variables, change is very possible and often likely.

Group Structure

As for group structure, this often is predetermined by the socioeconomic group we are born and raised in and the culture they reinforce or punish. By far, this is the parameter that is most often overcome by striving to move up the ladder of success by working hard and getting an education; and as we advance, so does our position within the social structure to reflect these achievements. Unfortunately, more individuals remain within their group of origin than leave it and adopt a more dominant or profitable group structure. I would imagine that this depends on the level of comfort one has within their current structure. Thus, if I feel that I am better than those in my current social group and feel that I don't belong there, I would be more inclined and motivated to migrate to other groups by engaging in the necessary behaviors to be accepted within that other group structure. Again, this will be highly influenced by our genetic predisposition as well as other factors such as opportunity and access to resources. Primarily, the motivation will come from within, as I hope to illustrate in later chapters. Whether I feel that I am better than others or not depends largely on how reciprocal my interactions are within the group and whether I get enough reinforcement from the group to keep me there. But as I mentioned in the opening remarks, the motivation to change and leave the current grouping depends on the internal feeling of comfort or discomfort of the organism relative to their position in the group structure. The more comfortable I am, the less likely I will try to change and move to a different grouping.

Cooperative Tendencies

Cooperative tendencies are highly dependent on group structure and depend, to a large degree, on accessibility to necessary resources. The very rich do not often seek out the poor to get into partnerships with them. They give those opportunities to those they know within their own group. There is much crossover in this area, but it is still much less than those that don't cross over. In fact, most of what are considered the higher classes have rules and social forces to specifically exclude those of the lower classes as depicted, for example, in the novel by Jane Austen, *Pride and Prejudice*. Although these social rituals and boundaries are not quite as clear or formalized in American culture, they do exist and are usually referred to as the old boys club that politicians and financial moguls develop to deal with their own and keep others out.

In short, many forces determine behaviors, only one of which is the environment. First and foremost, we are biological entities that are forever engaged in the pursuit of coming to terms with our frailties, our needs, and the behaviors we must engage in to survive. Overcoming or coming to terms with those needs in our everyday lives is a necessary endeavor of existence. In attempting to change them, and control them, we strive to have some unified approach, a frame of reference, a map that we can use, which works for us. By this I mean a working model of the world and how it works so that we can get it to work for us. We need to have it work for us because we need things from it for our own survival. The motivation to control our surroundings, our environment, is an obvious one. If we cannot control our environment enough to gain food and shelter from it, we may perish. But as we attempt to control our environment, our environment exerts control on us by its own physical limitations and constraints. There is reciprocity in our relationship with the environment between what we need from it and how we must behave to obtain it. Through cooperative efforts, we can alter the environment to be able to do things that we could not previously do, such as fly or travel underwater.

The Need to Know

Because it is impossible to survive in the world without procuring certain resources necessary for our survival—such as food, shelter, or health care—we develop a worldview or modus operandi to get those things from our environment, a loose system of rules and a general philosophy as to how things work. This view of the world begins to develop early in life, and at first is shaped by the parental unit, then by the larger social group, and finally by direct experience of what works for us. This progression shapes the ideas we have and assumptions we make about the world around us. Hopefully, this worldview improves our chance of survival in the world. The purpose of the current work is not to introduce any new scientific discoveries or present facts that have never been presented, nor is it an attempt to reinvent the wheel. What I will attempt is simply to point out relationships that have sprung out from my experience that show how these relationships, although not directly observable or measurable, can be instrumental in a functional analysis of behavior. There is nothing new about this finding, but rather, the conclusion reached may be, especially in the field of applied behavior analysis, novel to some to strictly adhere to the behavioral literature. These conclusions have revealed themselves through many years of experience in working with the developmentally disabled population, previous concepts I have studied, methods and research that I have had the opportunity to engage in, and looking at them through the eyes and theoretical structure provided to me through my educational and reinforcement history in the field while working with real people exhibiting real problems.

What I will attempt to do in the following chapters is present an *experiential* model of human behavior that can coexist with the principles of applied behavior analysis, but which also delve in the realm of the private world that we cannot directly observe and measure. Skinner spent much time and effort to explain and account for what he called *controlling variables*, private events, and the realm of thinking, using a behavioral terminology. Although he acknowledged the existence of this inner world, he objected to its place in the scientific explanation of behaviors. For him, if it was not an objective phenomenon that could be demonstrated by others, replicated, measured, and manipulated, then it was just an interesting concept, but not one that can be effectively used in the science of behavior, nor was it necessary to explain behavior. Although I don't disagree with any of his findings concerning the science of behavior as he saw it, I do take issue with not including these private events as an integral part of a functional analysis in the practical use of this technology. And I equally disagree with the notion that motivation comes from outside the organism as the more recent concept of *motivational operations* suggests. A motivational operation (also called an establishing operation) is anything that establishes conditions that improve the effectiveness of a reinforcer. For example, food is more reinforcing when the subject is hungry. Thus, food deprivation is a motivational operation. Deprivation imposed from outside the organism alters the probability that the subject will be motivated by food. The behavioral process is here defined without resorting to the inner event of hunger, which, I would argue, is not necessarily imposed from outside the organism, but, rather, as a result of the biophysiological construction of the subject being studied. Hunger will occur on its own with or without the imposition of deprivation from the environment. After a full meal, most organisms will self-impose deprivation by not eating until hunger occurs again. Hopefully, I will be able to make the case for including these inner events as part of a functional analysis in light of the fact that a functional analysis is itself an evolutionary process that changes with time, level of deprivation, and setting. In my view, as Skinner attempted to explain, there is no dualism. In this, we agree. The laws governing what we see are also the laws of those things we cannot see. When we consider the spectrum of sound or light, we can understand that although we only perceive a small slice of that spectrum, it does not mean that the areas of the spectrum that we cannot see operate under different laws of physics (see fig. 1). In the same way, the rules that govern our public behavior are also the rules that govern our private behavior. Skinner suggests this much in his *Science and Human Behavior*. It is a continuum that is not violated. Although we cannot prove this fact, there is no evidence to prove otherwise. In fact, there is much evidence that points in the direction of consistency and sameness rather than discontinuity and multiple and qualitatively different systems of causation.

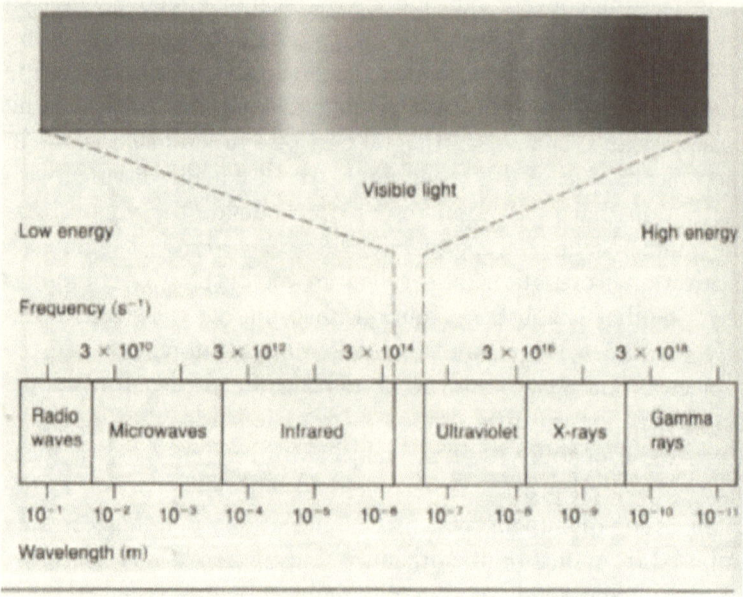

Figure 1: Visible light and the spectrum of light

In summary, I wish for the reader to understand that this is *not* a rebuttal of behaviorism but quite the contrary. I deeply believe in the principles of behaviorism. These principles have been substantiated in thousands of experiments, including my own research, and demonstrated in hundreds of different species of organisms. The laws of behaviorism are the same throughout, and the facts cannot be disputed. In my early research years, I actually demonstrated that the Freudian defense mechanism of "displacement activity" actually operated in fish (unpublished work, 1973). But applied behavior analysis, like anything else, is an evolving practice and application of behavioral principles hopefully to the point of describing not only observable events, but also unobservable events.

By its relentless pursuit to study only those parameters that we can see and manipulate, behaviorism has left out an essential aspect of human existence. A parameter that has been shown to play a very major role in the motivation of human behavior. That parameter is *emotion*. When someone resorts to the old saying "Love is blind," they are doing so to explain behavior that otherwise would seem improbable but for the special relationship that one has with someone else and the *feeling* they have for that individual. I need not enumerate the hundreds, if not thousands, of examples of behavior that appear to be totally irrational in our everyday existence but can be understood only in reference to the existence of an emotion. Love is indeed a very baffling emotion, but within the framework of hedonism, which I will discuss more fully in the next chapter, it is easy to see why a very rich man may jeopardize or simply give away large portions of his estate to a young girl who does not even appear to be intelligent enough to manage that kind of wealth. To that man, money is irrelevant; but feeling good in the presence of that individual is not. Being cognizant of one's mortality and the inability to take your money with you render large fortunes irrelevant. However, making the little time left on earth enjoyable is worth millions! Literally! And what is *enjoyable*? It is simply an emotion that feels good. It is something we all want more of, if possible, and we will work to get it when we know how.

The Search for Truth

I have come to accept the fact that truth can, and does, come in various forms. No particular modality of discovery has a monopoly on truth. Thus, truth may be derived at by the following:

- *science*, and the empirical approach that behaviorism offers, when it comes to understanding human behavior
- *experience*, especially those moments that don't occur often in our lives but result in significant change in our perception of the world

- *cognition* or logic, as in religion or philosophy, which can be strong forces in arousing emotions and unifying our experience as a people, and resulting in significant changes in behavior when applied systematically

All three have taught me why I behave and how to interpret that behavior. They all point to what is important and what is not. As mentioned above, attempting to make sense of our world and existence is an essential exercise of being. Thus, we are all looking for that "truth" and are developing it as we experience life and its consequences. And because we each experience life a little differently, the divide can be significant at times. This is what forces us to think differently and push our understanding to a more inclusive level, one that includes the views of others and experiences we have not had previously. When you have been exposed to a great deal of experiences of others, you begin to see beyond those differences and begin seeing the similarities. That is the principle of *generalization* in behaviorism. In philosophy, it is the realization that the universe is an undifferentiated aesthetic continuum. In Buddhism, it is achieving satori, or nirvana in Hinduism. And in the Jewish-Christian tradition, it is called being one with God. Basically, it is an emotion, a feeling that one understands the world and our place in it. In each case, the attempt is to see the unity and oneness of the universe by studying and describing its parts or, more accurately, the relationships of its parts. Somehow, anyone who has put any effort in thinking and explaining this issue to others has always spoken from an implied "wholeness" of the universe—meaning that there seems to be a constancy about our universe, and the more we know about its laws, the more we can control it and have it serve our purpose, namely, survival. And that drive to survive resides in us all, and we can't get rid of it. We must come to terms with it. We must meet its requirement and, often, exceed that requirement, sometimes by obscene amounts so that our offspring are assured dominance in the scheme of things far into the future. This restlessness is a form of anxiety that drives us all. For some, that anxiety produces volumes of works, great efforts in the understanding and domination of our universe, driven by an insecurity that we will surely perish; and controlling our world is a way of assuring survival and delaying that prospect. In many philosophies, this relentless and constant pursuit of understanding of the world "out there" has blinded many by the force within driving all of this behavior. An inner restlessness that requires soothing. And to find that soothing, we behave.

CHAPTER 3

Behavioral Sociobiology as Worldview

In attempting to describe any parameter of human existence, one must come to terms with the world around us. One develops assumptions and beliefs about how things work through experiences that color their view of that world. For example, if you come from a hostile family in a hostile neighborhood and have had some bad experiences of bullies taking your lunch money at school, you are likely to view the world in a much more negative way than, say, the rich kid that gets whatever he wants. That bias of one's own peculiar and unique experience has been the source of serious disagreements among us. Attempts to transcend this bias have been attempted by the concept of *scientific objectivity* and empiricism. These concepts are the rules of engagement, so to speak, for proposing certain courses of action that will affect not only the person making them, but all others within that social structure. Theories of reality and the universe are as plentiful as there are people in the world. However, societies cannot advance or even exist without some form of agreement among its members about what is and is not beneficial to the group as a whole. Thus, it has always been important for information to be corroborated by others. Before science, the most popular form of validation was one's personal experience. And the higher your place in society, the more weight your personal views had on your social structure. However, as we all know, different experiences will inevitably lead to different conclusions.

How, then, could we develop a set of laws that we can all live by if any one of us can come up with our own rules based on our own experience, which may not be shared by the larger community? Inevitably, there will arise disagreements, dissension, and the splitting of factions based on belief systems. This is what occurred in the history of religions. Even when we use the same facts and events to prove our point, it is the *interpretation* of those facts that troubles us. So we needed something more reliable. Something that we could all agree on. This consensus among us has not happened, as you can see just by listening to the news or even just by talking to your neighbors and friends about politics or religion. And I am not arrogant enough to suggest that I will lay all of this discord to rest.

The search for truth has been the preoccupation of man (and women) for thousands of years. Prior to science, it was religion and philosophy. These systems prescribe a way of viewing and understanding the world around us. The importance of adhering to a particular view has inherent implications. For example, if you believe that teaching kids to read is a dangerous thing and should not be taught until they are adults, then in constructing a society that must get along with each other, you would demand that no child be taught to read until they reach adulthood. So living within a social structure, which all of us do, we have to agree on some basic guidelines that are often determined by our culture, which then turn into laws; and these laws must then be enforced. Hence, the importance of a worldview that we can agree on. If not all of us, then at least most of us. Societies are theoretically built with the guiding principle of producing an environment that achieves the greatest good for the greatest number.

A unifying worldview is inescapable to anyone interested in the world around us. There does, indeed, appear to be some logical and coherent set of laws and consistent relations that exist in the world, which cannot be violated; but as we all know, there are exceptions to every rule. But even those exceptions require a certain set of parameters and variables to exist for their occurrence. However, once those rules have been agreed upon, they make our world more predictable, more controllable, and allow us to extract from it the things we need to survive. Sociobiology is such a worldview, as are all others, from psychoanalysis to physics, from numerology to behaviorism, from paganism to Christianity. In every case, these worldviews attempt to present the world and all of its complexities in an orderly manner that explains our experience in it. For many, this is impossible to do in the natural world, and they resort to supernatural forces to account for the immense complexities of the human experience. Religions, philosophies, schools of thought, even witchcraft, voodoo, and Greek mythology are all such systems to describe the world and our place in it. For some of these worldviews, one is required to have faith, meaning that they must believe even in the absence of any evidence to support the conclusions that they are required to believe in. In others, one must have evidence. And still for others, it requires extrapolation, whereby what applies in one situation is presumed to act in other situations in a similar manner, even in the absence of evidence that such a relationship exists. For me, the primary criterion rests on two main requirements:

1. That the worldview is consistent with my experience of life
2. That the assumptions that I make in relation to this view can be predicted in a consistent way, even though it may not be observed, measured, or manipulated in any objective way

Worldviews are necessary for us to make sense out of our experiences. For example, behaviorism believes that behaviors are the product of their environment and the consequences that result from interacting with that environment. That view has been experimentally demonstrated over and over. Yet many people still doubt that behaviorism is the right worldview. I myself am suggesting that there is more to it, and I am a behavioral psychologist. The fact of the matter is that any relationships that have been discovered and manipulated effectively are part of the ultimate truth and must be included in any credible worldview. If science has achieved anything in the past two thousand years, it is that the world, and even the universe, functions according to certain relationships that are lawful, predictable, and to some degree controllable, but *not* alterable. This is why magic fascinates us; it seems to defy the laws of nature. The operative word here is *seems* because, once revealed, there is no fascination with the outcome observed. I can change someone's behavior, but I cannot do so without following the general principles of behavior change.

The laws of the universe are incredibly stable and, once discovered, become predictable. So if I know that a hurricane is coming, I can get out of its way, but I cannot stop it. But who knows, maybe we will discover the laws of hurricanes and are eventually able to stop them. Science has not advanced to that level yet. We can't even cure the common cold, AIDS, or many forms of cancer!

Science has proven itself to be one of the most fruitful worldviews that we have discovered thus far, at least in the realm of manipulating our physical environment. It is the discovered laws of science that allows us to fly in big steel and metal vehicles, breathe underwater with tanks, and make drugs that can alter our experience of reality. The laws of science are such that they are incremental in their products and accessible to anyone. The same cannot be said about philosophy, religion, and theory. Those are the guidelines for science. Science is simply a methodology of discovering underlying principles, consistent facts, relationships that can be duplicated and predicted, etc., where theory, philosophy, and religion provide the direction that science should be moving toward and investigating. Only through investigation, experimentation, and close scrutiny can we be sure that our assumptions are correct. Einstein said, "God does not play dice with the universe!" If your assumptions are correct, the outcome should reflect that.

The Need for Science: A Brief History

The development of the scientific method has been around a long time. Ancient Egyptian documents, such as early papyri, describe methods of medical diagnosis. The Greeks described the method of empiricism. The first experimental scientific method was developed by a Muslim scientist who introduced the use of experimentation and quantification to evaluate competing scientific theories within an empirical orientation that emerged with Alhazen's optical experiments in his *Book of Optics* (1021). The modern scientific method was further refined in the seventeenth and eighteenth centuries. In his work *Novum Organum* (1620)—a reference to Aristotle's *Organon*—Francis Bacon outlined a system of logic that improves on the old philosophical process of syllogism. Then in 1637, René Descartes established the framework for a scientific method's guiding principles in his treatise, *Discourse on the Method*. The writings of Alhazen, Bacon, and Descartes are critical in the historical development of the modern scientific method.

Lundin (1979) outlined several historical antecedents to behaviorism. Aristotle, the most significant Greek naturalist, suggested the approach of objective and observable data as the basis of studying the human experience. Second, the French naturalists gravitated toward materialism and opposed spiritualism. Within this school, Julien Offray de La Mettrie developed the doctrine of hedonism, the concept that pleasure is the chief god of life. Then came Pierre Cabanis who based consciousness on the body since those who were beheaded via the guillotine were not conscious. And finally, Auguste Comte introduced the notion of positivism and further argued that only observable knowledge was valid. Third, animal psychology was gaining ground with all of its proponents defending the idea that man and beast represent a continuum of responding organisms with no gap. Hence the beginning of comparative psychology. Fourth, Pavlov's work on the conditioned reflex served as the basis for all kinds of learning and the mechanism by which behavior could be controlled and modified via discrete behavioral manipulations.

These antecedents, coupled with Watson's dislike of the functionalist school in which he had been entrenched, served as the background upon which Watson wrote "Psychology as the Behaviorist Views It," (1913). In this article, he argues for a purely objective experimental branch of natural science, and his view became known as the behaviorist's manifesto. For Watson, the behaviorist's goal is prediction and control of behavior. These ideas were later formulated in a book, perhaps his most significant, called *Psychology from the Standpoint of a Behaviorist* (Watson, 1919). Coupled with the work of Thorndike and the law of effect describing his satisfiers and annoyers as the fuel for learning, the stage was set for a formalized behaviorism.

It was against this backdrop that B. F. Skinner found himself in when he began one of the most ambitious experimental careers in the field of operant conditioning and in formalizing Thorndike's satisfiers and annoyers into reinforcement and punishment. One of his most important contributions was his description of different schedules of reinforcement and how these shape behavior. Thus, the field of psychology has now been transformed, at least partially, into an empirical, rather than a theoretical or conceptual, science.

It should be easy to see that the transformation described above to move toward an objective science came from the subjective contemplation and philosophical ideas that shaped them. When one accepts the one (objectivism) and rejects the other (subjectivism), one is in essence creating a dualism. For there is nothing in science that proves there is no importance or validity to subjective experience. Again, just because you cannot see it and control it does not mean it's not there. As I mentioned earlier, Skinner spent much time talking about these subjective events and making the case that regardless of what they are, they have no place in a scientific functional analysis of behavior. It is this one point that not only turns many people off to behaviorism but has also actually come to serious clashes with those that have religious beliefs that have never been accounted for but are experienced by many and whose behavior is determined by such emotional experiences and beliefs.

This clash between science and religion in recent years stems from the assumption that the two are incompatible. Because both claim to be telling the truth, some have concluded that both cannot be right and one has to choose between the two. However, proving anything in nature with science does not preclude the existence of other forces yet to be discovered. There is no law or principle of science that claims that what is known is all that will ever be known. As the French say, "Au contraire, mon frére." Science simply seeks to concern itself with objective data that can be proven, duplicated, and corroborated by any who wish to investigate it. It does not claim that if you cannot see it, then it doesn't exist. We know that to be false from studies in physics, chemistry, and many other fields of study.

There are many things that we can measure and manipulate that we cannot see. Science does, however, reject explanations of phenomenon that cannot be demonstrated in the manner stated above. Thus, until one can show the results of such manipulations, science is not interested. Again, I hope to blur that line in talking about advertising, politics, and the general human experience, where manipulation of information and focusing on peoples' emotions can indeed produce a measurable behavioral effect even if we cannot show emotion or the change in one's thinking as a result of listening to verbal information and seeing certain visual images.

My Worldview

In attempting to understand my own world, I have, as many others, arrived at a worldview that actually unites the seemingly irreconcilable differences of science and religion. Not that I have invented any new material or discovered some unknown mystery, but, rather, by structuring a view that is a unique arrangement of the facts that account for my experiences of the world as well as my academic training in the science of behavior, both in the field and experimentation in the laboratory.

My worldview is that the universe, as we know it, is one unified system that functions like a living organism with many parts, or like the human body with all of its organs and systems, and is responsive to the same set of laws and relationships throughout. Some of these laws and relationships can be and have been discovered and described to some degree. And once they have been discovered, they have proved to be predictable and can be used to further advance our ability to use them to sustain ourselves and protect us from the environment's more dangerous aspects that can be quite harmful to frail organisms such as ourselves. I believe that the best way to reveal and discover these laws, forces, and relationships is through the scientific model of inquiry, primarily empiricism, and the use of methods based on observation and experimentation.

However, I also believe that experience offers additional data that is very much inaccessible to science at the present time and that neither behaviorism nor any other forms of science to date have been able to account for objectively. Yet experience is as real to each one of us as any objective reality out there that we can touch or manipulate. In fact, one's experiences and how one feels are often the most important factors that determine how one will behave. Thus, it is essential that we deal with these unknown forces in a methodical way, if such a way can be described in some coherent and logical fashion. I believe that this is a vacuum in today's behaviorism, one that I hope to focus on and provide some ideas that may be later tested for accuracy and consistency to further the science of behavior. I myself have not spent much time in the laboratory recently, and most of what I am attempting to share in this treatment of behaviorism are the results of direct experience in the field. And it is that field that has shaped my worldview to where it is today.

Because I have almost exclusively worked with the developmentally disabled population, I have had to deal with the limitations of the cognitive processes so popular in psychology and focus much more on physiological disturbances that seem responsible for a great deal of inappropriate behaviors. I have discovered that it is not necessarily the physical limitations that produce the behavioral problems, but, rather, how the environment has reacted to those limitations by assuming that those with limitations cannot do *anything*. When the average person passes by a developmentally disabled person in a wheelchair, unable to talk or indicate their needs to others, it is often assumed that they are devoid of feelings, unaware of our conversations about them when we talk about them, as if they were not even there, or simply view them as nonthinking and nonfeeling individuals. Careful observation of their behaviors would lead us to completely different conclusions. However, this sociological situation provokes emotional changes in the disabled individual that, while not directly measurable, can be observed in facial changes, level of responsiveness, and other behavioral symptoms, which can only be repaired in the normal way we do with each other, by showing affection, attending to their needs, and empathizing with their condition. When that is implemented, the individual often reacts with increased responsiveness, fewer behavioral problems, and a greater willingness to learn, perform, and strive to achieve more in their lives.

The process described above is rooted in our own emotional bias. Regardless of educational knowledge or religious belief, our emotional bias is shaped very early in life. How we respond to "outsiders" is something we feel internally as an emotion of fear, and we tend to shy away from things that make us fearful. Thus, when we have been raised to fear others that do not look like us, live like us, or believe like us, we tend to see those "others" as something less than ourselves. Thus, when we are confronted with them, we assume that they are not like us and are baffled by what makes them tick. As mentioned above, we are all a little bit different, and we are all a little bit alike. So when one enters into an interaction with someone else that is seemingly very different, they focus on this difference to validate their own bias and misconception and pay little attention to the commonalities. It would be frightening to think that this individual whom you have been taught for years that is different from you is actually a lot like you. And it is largely this emotional reaction that guides our perception of that individual, and we tend to validate that perception by anything that individual does that we would not do. If we approached even people in our families with that sort of bias, we could justify that they are not like us either. This is the root of racism, discrimination, and the persecution of others and has much to do with our misconceived need to survive and dominate others to do so, as if that is the only option. I suggest that it is not, and in fact, it is the wrong option. The prostitute and the drug dealer need food, shelter, and love every bit as much as the pastor, the teacher, and the developmentally disabled person.

Granted that these emotional variables cannot be directly observed, measured, or manipulated in a controlled manner. But influencing and changing such emotions can be observed, and the behavioral benefits of such changes are often extremely significant. Taking those variables into account is one of the major points of my worldview. Just because one cannot objectively observe a reality that we all experience does not necessitate the total disregard of that parameter, which can be shown to have an effect on behavior. Again, experience says it does indeed exist and is the driving force of much observable behavior. As I hope to illustrate in the pages ahead, the concept of *emotion* should not be disregarded when dealing with human behavior. However, in a purely behavioristic approach, that is exactly what is done. Not because behaviorists don't believe that emotions exist, but because they insist on dealing strictly with behaviors and variables that are directly observable and measurable. While I agree that we should stick to this rule as much as possible, I believe that emotions are too important a variable influencing behavior change to be ignored. And it is too valuable a resource to overlook. Thus, I will attempt to describe how emotions affect our behavior and how they can fit into a functional analysis. I will also attempt to standardize or formalize observations of emotions as part of the functional analysis so as to derive workable and effective behavior intervention plans.

In summary, it is my worldview that we are biological entities with requirements—requirements that are experienced as emotions and must be met only by behaving, and in behaving, we must come to terms with our specific social structure. Hence *behavioral sociobiology*.

CHAPTER 4

In the Beginning: Why We Behave

To understand why we behave, let us first describe some obvious parameters affecting our behaviors. The human experience can be characterized as a state of constant vacillation between periods of biological disequilibrium and equilibrium. These seemingly opposite states are experienced in the organism as emotional states that range from contentment to anxiety. From the moment that we are born until the moment we expire, we are in a constant state of behaving. As soon as we are out of the womb, we are compelled to behave. Why, you may ask, must we behave? The obvious observable fact as to why we behave is that it is necessary for survival. One must breathe to survive. Breathing is a behavior. Luckily for us, we come into the world with a few automatic behaviors or behaviors that don't have to be taught, which we call *reflexes*, such as breathing, sucking, or grasping; and these help us to behave in such a way as to be able to eat to sustain ourselves, but not much more. From that point on and the rest of the organism's life, the necessity and drive to survive will be dealt with by learning new behaviors that will assure that outcome and prolong the inevitable end of that organism's existence on the planet. This process is inevitable; it happens to all species of biological existence, including animals and plants alike. In fact, it could be argued that this process reaches far beyond our planet. This birth and death cycle ensures that the universe remains new and vibrant, constantly evolving and adapting to the changing forces in the environment—forces that we have barely begun to understand, chronicle, or measure.

The essential and important nature of behavior is such that it cannot be overlooked. As we shall see, the misapplication of behavioral principles can turn a bad situation to something much worse if not used and applied appropriately. Thus, it is essential that we understand everything we can about it. I begin here by setting the stage and attempting to answer the first question about behavior, namely, why do we behave?

Let us begin by referencing observable behavior with known biological facts. The child, when first born, does not know it is hungry or it is cold or who it is that is looking at them. But in most instances, the baby cries. If it doesn't cry, it is stimulated, then reacts to the stimulation by crying. Crying appears to be a reflexive reaction to discomfort. A reflex is, by definition, a behavior that occurs without any prior learning. However, as soon as the environment begins to react to the crying baby by doing something to the baby, the learning process has begun. Every consequence of the environment on the child's behavior from then on will be part of their reinforcement history and will affect future behavior. I will discuss reinforcement later, but for now, we simply mean that as the environment reacts to the baby, the baby begins to react to the environment.

The Principle of Reciprocity

I saw a cartoon once where two gorillas were talking to each other while in a cage with a depiction of a scientist a short distance away outside the cage, wearing a white coat and a with clipboard in hand, and one gorilla says to the other gorilla, "Watch this, I will get that guy with the white coat to give me a banana." In the second frame, you see the gorilla pulling a lever and the scientist coming over with the banana. This illustrates a very important principle that is not much talked about in behaviorism, the principle of *reciprocity* in behavior interactions. As we behave by acting on the environment, the environment influences our responses either by reacting in the way we intend for it to react, thus reinforcing our behavior, or by not reacting in the way we wanted it to react, thus motivating us to act or behave differently to achieve our desired result. Picture organisms as clay and the environment as the artist's hand. As the artist shapes the clay, the clay alters the artist's hand by sticking to it, eroding the skin, and making the artist tired, thereby altering the hand's behavior. This *reciprocity* occurs at many different levels, and in every science. For every action, there is a reaction. For every reaction, there is another reaction, and so forth. What we shall see later on is that this principle of *reciprocity* requires that to change behavior in others, our own behavior must be changed. There is a feedback loop that is in constant motion from one subject to the other subject and back, endlessly for the duration of any interaction. Thus, intervention is more an art form rather than a science, and the precision of science is not necessary for a successful outcome in the natural world. It is only important in the laboratory and when we are in need to prove a point or relationship. In experience, it is mainly the result that matters.

This balancing act of give-and-take can be more formalized by the following illustration. The illustration below (fig. 2) depicts a theoretical *resting state*, which actually does not exist but is only a concept of a state of being that is free of needs, drives, purpose, or discomfort. It is a state of total contentment. However, given that biological entities are *never* at rest, this is only a theoretical state that is actually taught in certain sects and religions such as yogis and maharishis in India. Carlos Castaneda, in his series of books on Mexican *brujos* (witch doctors), called it "making the world stop," and it was a goal to be achieved in the training, not something that is experienced by biological entities naturally (*A Separate Reality*, 1971). Thus, the *resting state* is one of no motivation, and this condition rarely happens in the human experience.

When the organism is in the resting state, or close to it, the organism does not behave much. The organism is not seeking any manipulation of the environment, is not attempting to escape pain, and is not seeking pleasure. However, in time, certain needs arise, motivation increases, and behavior must occur once again. Thus, the sheer passage of time results in deficit states. So you should look at the illustration below with the resting state being a timeline that affects deficit states in that order. It is consistent and predictable. For example, you *will* eventually get thirsty, become motivated to act, and eventually drink, thus reducing your deficit state of thirst. It is not essential to know exactly how many hours it would take to make you thirsty, but we know you will be thirsty eventually as time passes and the cycle is repeated.

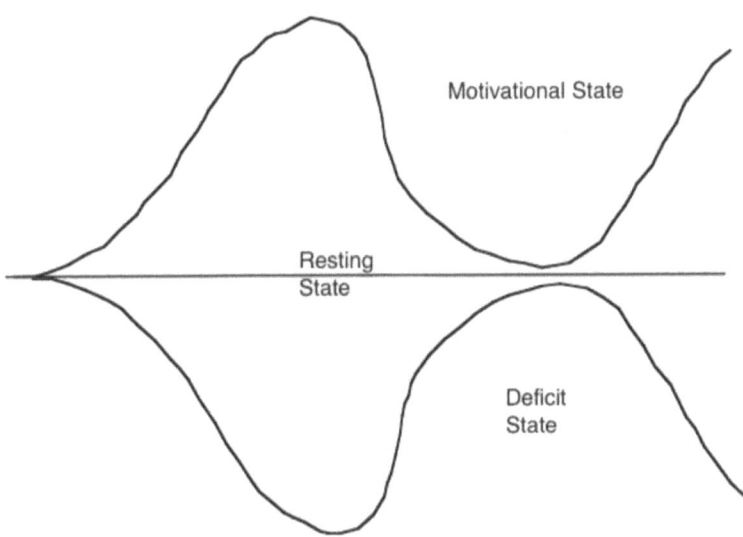

Figure 2: The relation between deprivation and
motivation

Thus, although we cannot definitively quantify this relationship—the equation that would determine the degree of correlation between the deprivation and motivation objectively—it has been determined experimentally that to some degree, as the deprivation increases, so does the degree of motivation to act unless, of course, the deprivation is too much and actually threatens the existence of the organism experiencing it. Simply stated, as the organism's needs increase, their motivation to behave to alleviate that need also increases. And by the same reasoning, as the level of need is reduced, the motivation to behave to continue to reduce the need decreases. For example, if I am in a meeting that I expected to last an hour, and the meeting was held toward the end of the day, say at 4:00 PM, and I would expect to get out at 5:00 PM around my dinnertime, I would not be eating too many doughnuts and drinking coffee for fear of spoiling my appetite. Now let's say that complications occurred during the meeting and various people present could not agree on an appropriate course of action for the issue at hand and two hours passed with no end in sight. Given that I usually eat dinner at around 5:00 PM and it is already 6:00 PM, those doughnuts are beginning to look good. I may even break my own desire not to spoil my appetite and eat one. In this situation, my motivation to act on my hunger increased, leading to increased motivation to behave to alleviate that hunger and engage in behavior I did not originally want to engage in. The tipping point for when I will violate the rule is simply a matter of variation in time.

The Body Talking

If one were to analyze one's own behavior in the previous situation, one can see that the body communicates to us all the time. Needs, which are inescapable, particularly the need for food and drink, are communicated to our bodies through the feeling of discomfort or experience of disequilibrium. Deficit states trigger biochemical events that alter our chemistry and result in emotional changes that affect how we feel at that moment. If the lack of food continues, the discomfort will begin to make noise to further attempt to focus our attention on the problem. And if this situation continues, we may feel dizzy, weak, and may even start shaking. These internally provoked responses continue until we either remedy the situation or pass out.

> Experiments performed on human subjects show that the production of appetites and affects is not limited to the core-brain mechanisms. Appetitive and affective interest is more generally aroused whenever the interrelationships among neural logic structures anywhere in the brain are disturbed. A cybernetic theory of motivation and emotion develops from neurophysiological experiments that detail the control of these relationships exerted by the brain cortex. (Languages of the brain, Englewood, New Jersey, Pribram, 1971)

Pribram is talking about the internal cues that translate into emotional experience that eventually, when strong enough, move the individual to do something about their state of discomfort. Failure to act will result in a chronic condition of discomfort. When the organism is not at ease, they are in dis-ease. And the prolonged effect of dis-ease is disease. This occurs because when we are not at ease, we are burning up precious biological and immune system resources that could be helping us but are now only agitating us and burning up our energy, further reducing our ability to fight bacteria.

Although I am talking about obvious needs that are usually used in experimental situations in the laboratory, because they are always effective in motivating behavior, I am suggesting that the same process is occurring with the need for affection, the need to escape boredom, the need to procreate, the need to feel important to others, and the need to be safe. This last need can be further subdivided into several categories such as physical safety by living in an acceptable neighborhood, financial safety such as having some money in the bank in the event of an emergency or if you lose your job, and social safety by having friends that are supportive in case you need help. Thus, the hypothetical graph depicted above can be multiplied many times over (see fig. 3) for all of the possible needs that we are capable of experiencing. It is hypothesized from this view that behavior will be determined by the need that is most pressing at the time. Thus, if you are freezing and hungry and you can only eat by standing outside at the hot dog stand, you will endure the cold and eat if that need is more pressing than your comfort. You may, on the other hand, forgo eating until it's warmer outside or until you get to a place that is warm because your need for comfort is greater than your need for food. Let us be clear here that when we are talking about having a need, or being hungry or thirsty, we are talking about emotions that are biochemically mediated within a social structure that must be navigated to alter itself. We must behave within the social structure to procure those things that will calm or change that emotion or feeling that is making us restless and uncomfortable. Behavior serves to bring out that balance by finding whatever it is that was needed.

The Gradient Effect

In talking about needs and emotions, it is not the presence or absence of hunger, thirst, or some other emotion. In just about everything encountered in the natural world, we see that although things look like they oppose each other—such as light and

51

darkness, fast and slow, or satiation and deprivation—these are not two distinct things out there that can be pointed to but, rather, extreme degrees of the same thing. Thus, needs are at the low end of an individual's resources while satiation is at the high end of having those resources. In most situations, the visible part of any need does not represent the range of that need. As I mentioned earlier about the light spectrum, we are only able to see a small portion of it (see fig. 1 above).

Kahlil Gibran, a famous Lebanese poet, wrote in *The Prophet*,

> And one of the elders of the city said,
> "Speak to us of Good and Evil."
> And he answered:
> Of the good in you I can speak, but not
> Of the evil.
> For what is evil but good tortured by its
> Own hunger and thirst?
> Verily when good is hungry it seeks food
> Even in dark caves, and when it thirsts it
> Drinks even of dead waters.

When discussing any parameter influencing human behavior, or behavior in general, we are always talking about a hypothetical place on a hypothetical gradient. We experience gustatory discomfort ranging from severe hunger to being too full after a big meal. Motivation, pertaining to this particular need or any other, is to have enough food that you are not hungry, and not too much food that you are uncomfortably full. It is hypothesized that this motivational model is the same for all possible needs that one can experience. Thus, the graph above can be viewed as representing one particular need while the actual experience of the individual is more like that in figure 3 below. At any moment, one state of discomfort can overshadow or surpass another in a constant state of flux.

The view of the biologist is largely a structural one based on empirical observation of the internal interactions between living matter and chemical structures that are "inside" the organism. Behaviorism deals with the results of what that biology produces "outside" the organism in the form of expressed behaviors with the goal to achieve *discomfort reduction* or *need reduction* within a social structure that can help or hinder that effort. However, the third and most important parameter for the organism is their experience of this interplay between biology and its behavior in a social structure with other organisms. It is this experience that I want to address more directly within a behavioral framework since I believe that it has been lacking in the field of applied behavior analysis. This is the essence of what I view as a *behavioral sociobiology*.

Experience appears to vacillate somewhere between contentment, which is static in its character, and anxiety, which is dynamic in character. In contentment, you feel in control; but in anxiety, you feel out of control. In other words, we are maximally motivated to change through behavior when we are anxious, and least motivated to change when content. M. S. Peck, the author of *The Road Less Traveled*, once said, "The truth is that our finest moments are most likely to occur when we are feeling deeply uncomfortable, unhappy, or unfulfilled. For it is only in such moments, propelled by our discomfort, that we are likely to step out of our ruts and start searching for different ways or truer answers."

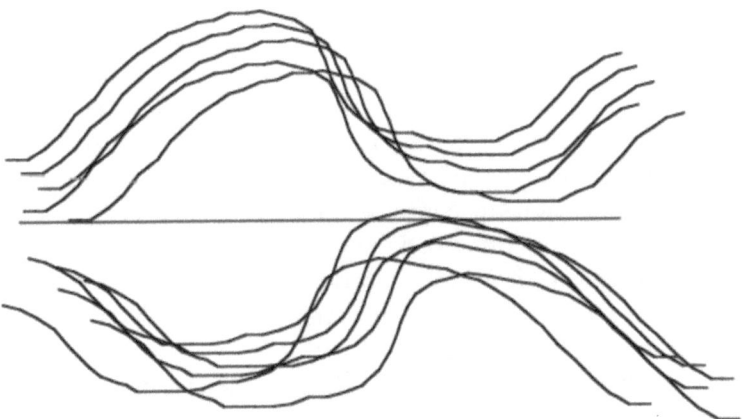

Figure 3: The interplay of several need
states and motivation

Deficit states, which are inevitable to any living form, produce changes in the biochemistry of the organism, such that it alerts the individual via a chemical and physiological change that is not comfortable for the organism, to alert them that they must *do something*. There is uneasiness about them. They are not content and not at rest. They become restless and seek a solution to their discomfort. It is this feeling of a deficit within us that motivates all behavior. When we are completely content, we do very little in the way of behavior. We can simply sit and experience our existence and its beauty. When we are not in that place, we behave in such a way as to find ourselves back there or closer to that point of contentment. For example, if we want to see a lot of animal behavior at the zoo, the time to visit is *not* right after the animals eat. Usually, they are at rest, and maybe even napping. Rather, it is the time just prior to eating when the motivational states are at their highest point. Thus, although I cannot measure or see hunger in animals, if I know their feeding schedule, I can predict the best time to observe their behavior. In this case, I am predicting behavior based on a presumed schedule of needs that cannot be observed or measured, but, nevertheless, can be accurate enough to yield good results, namely, to see the animals behaving rather than napping.

It can be argued that we spent the majority of our life either working our way up to the resting state or working our way down to the resting state. For example, if you had to work on Christmas Day in a local grocery store for eight hours, and within those eight hours not a single customer came in, you would probably be bored. Your need for quiet and rest is no longer important, and your need for excitement and action are activated. So as soon as you get off your shift, you begin seeking some stimulation and change in your behavioral pattern. This is working your way up to the resting state. On the other hand, let's say you worked on a Saturday night in the emergency room of a hospital in a large metropolitan city with a high crime rate. You would probably experience more action there than you would probably prefer. Thus, at the end of your shift, your need for excitement is quite low, and your need for rest is high. So as soon as you go off your shift, you will be seeking a place and an activity that is calmer and more relaxed. In this case, you are working your way down to the resting state.

This on-and-off pattern is replicated over and over, but not necessarily for the same need. We all get hungry, then get full, then get hungry again. In the same way, we might need a friend, then need to be left alone, then need a friend again. And as mentioned above, the behavior we engage in will be the one that most directly addresses the greatest need of the moment. This is not a new idea. Bozarth (1994) said the following in his article on the pleasure systems of the brain:

> Much of behavior can be explained by simple processes of approaching pleasant stimuli and avoiding painful stimuli as described by Spencer (1880) in the nineteenth century. The ventral tegmental dopamine system is an important neural substrate for reward, and it has a central role in regulating appetitive motivation: several distinct rewarding events activate this reward system, and activation of this system elicits appetitive motivation. The ventral tegmental dopamine system, along with its various neural inputs and outputs, can be aptly designated a "pleasure system in the brain" with an important role regulating many normal and pathological behaviors. (M. A. Bozarth, "Pleasure Systems in the Brain," ed. D. M. Warburton, *Pleasure: The Politics and the Reality* [New York: John Wiley & Sons, 1994], 5–14+refs, Note: Minor typographical errors appearing in the published version have been corrected.)

We can see from the previous quote that this idea has been around since the 1800s. Indeed, much earlier in Greek mythology, Dionysus was the god of song, wine, and women, born from the thigh of Zeus. He became associated with hedonism, the practice of seeking pleasure and avoiding pain.

Hedonism

Democritus (c. 460 BC to c. 370 BC), a materialist philosopher also known as the Laughing Philosopher, believed that all matter is made up of various imperishable, indivisible elements that he called *atoma*, or indivisible units, from which we get the English word *atom*. He seems to be the earliest philosopher on record to have categorically embraced a hedonistic philosophy; he called the supreme goal of life as contentment, or cheerfulness, claiming that "joy and sorrow are the distinguishing mark of things beneficial and harmful."

These ideas of pleasure and pain can be viewed as the predecessors of Thorndike's satisfiers and annoyers and, later, Skinner's operant conditioning with its reinforcement theory. Thus, there is nothing new about this "pleasure principle," as Freud called it. Human experience tells us that no one seeks painful stimuli unless it leads to more intense pleasure. James Olds and Peter Milner (1954), two investigators at McGill University, were studying learning and how stimulation of the brain interacted with such learning. They planted electrodes with a stereotaxic apparatus into what they thought would be the appropriate placement in the rat's brain. After preliminary experimentation with manually stimulating the rat's brain, they provided the rat with a lever to press that would produce this brain stimulation at will. The rat quickly learned to press the lever repeatedly. If given a choice between stimulation and food to a hungry rat, the rat would still prefer the stimulation (see fig. 4 below).

One can interpret these results in several ways. However, I prefer to present my own interpretation rather than enumerate those interpretations offered by others. In a nutshell, it *is* hedonism.

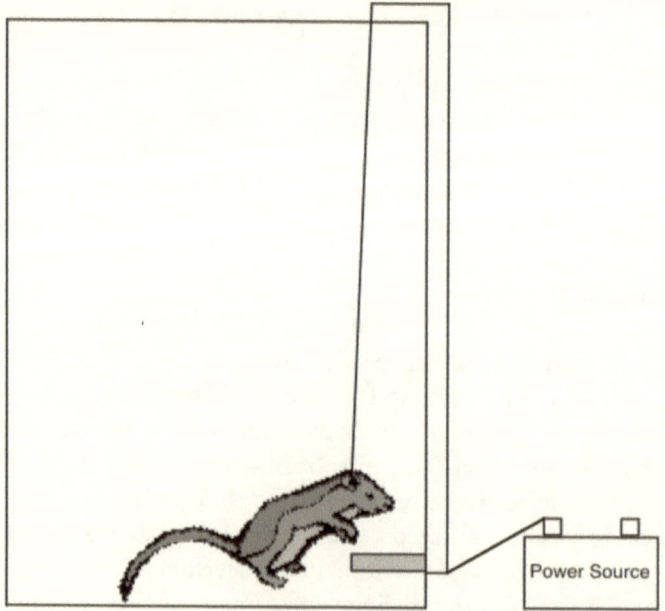

Figure 4: A rat stimulating himself by pressing on a lever

What motivates the rat to behave and keeps him behaving are the emotions he experiences when he presses that lever. We all want to feel good, and if we find something that makes us feel good, we are motivated to repeat that behavior. Sounds a lot like the behavioral theory of reinforcement. The difference is, of course, that while all environmental reinforcers are *not* shared by all organisms and vary a great deal depending on the current state of deprivation, this type of direct neurological reinforcement works on all humans and animals alike that we have tested without any state of deprivation. There is much research available in this field that is beyond the scope of this book, but I simply want to make the case that feeling good is a prime universal motivator. And the physiology of biological entities are designed in such a way as to not only make us uncomfortable when deficit states arise and needs increase, but also to inform us as to what is the good and appropriate response to make to lower the intensity of the discomfort and increase the feeling and emotion of contentment when we engage in the behavior that is appropriate to reduce the deficit state. This is what we think of as bringing ourselves back into balance—to replenish what has been depleted, whether it's food, water, cold, or heat. When there are no needs that are being neglected, no pain to come to terms with, etc., and we feel fine, then we are temporarily in balance. Keeping us in balance is the subject matter of hundreds of systems that teach ways of doing just that. The current work is no different in its aim.

A word of caution on the "feeling good" mantra is in order here. Just because something feels good does not necessarily mean that it is good for you. Think of fattening foods, illicit drugs, promiscuous sexual contacts, etc., to name a few. This is where the cognitive processes must work to override the biochemical and physiological preferences of the organism. Close scrutiny will reveal that some of these things that make us feel good have long-term negative effects and thus should be avoided or used sparingly.

In summary, to answer the question as to why we behave, behavior is our only tool to survive. To survive, we must engage in certain behaviors on a regular basis, such as eating, drinking, defecating, and emptying our bladders only to repeat this endless process. To do those things, we must engage in behavior, but not just any behavior. We must engage in behavior that meets the requirements of our particular sociobiological need at that moment and continue to do so from moment to moment until we expire. Behaviors are provoked, emitted, and reinforced only to the extent that they meet this requirement. Meeting that requirement means that they make us feel good, or at least better than we did when we had the need. That is the chief effect of reinforcement. In fact, as I will discuss later about reinforcement, the only things that are reinforcing are the things that meet our need at the time and result in the cessation of discomfort or the feeling of contentment. Hence the biological basis of all behaviors.

CHAPTER 5

What Are Behaviors

According to applied behavior analysis, the definition of behavior is that it is simply anything that a person does or says. As I mentioned earlier, my view of behaviors is that they are our only tools to survive. In an effort to survive, we must do many things such as keeping ourselves safe, eating adequate amounts of nutrition, seeking a mate, procreating, protecting our young, etc. And to complicate things, these needs simply arise, independent of behavior, and on their own time schedule that is intimately tied to our biological state at the time. Thus, we may usually have lunch at around 12:30 PM, but I may experience hunger by 11:00 AM. The first rule, then, of our biology is that it varies from moment to moment and has much to do with various forces, all of which have some influence on what we perceive as our need at the time. Some of these influences are *physiological*. For example, when you will get hungry, it will depend on when you last ate, how much you ate, what you ate, how fast your metabolism is, how much energy you have been expending since that last meal, and so on. Some influences are *sociological*. For example, you may feel that you have to wait for your other partners or social group members to eat with you, and it would not be accepted if you just ate on your own. You may not be able to eat certain items that are fattening in front of your peers since you are already overweight and don't wish to give your peer group the wrong impression. Some of the influences can be *psychological*. For example, you may be having difficulty in your marriage and are preoccupied with how to handle the situation. This will, of course, have an impact on your behavior and daily routine. You may, on purpose, avoid social settings where you will have to engage in superficial small talk and seek a more solitary path; thus, you wind up eating in a place you don't even like but is far from your peer group.

Behaviors, then, are the responses we make that have the highest probability of meeting our momentary and long-range needs, at least according to our understanding of the situation at that time. As we shall see later, as we learn more, we are more likely to engage in behaviors that are more effective in meeting those needs. Behaviors are the fuel that gets us to where we need to be, primarily, to be free from discomfort. What responses we make will depend on various things. First and foremost, our previous history will determine which behavior we engage in, especially in previous times when we felt as we do at the moment. Whatever we did then to escape the feeling we are experiencing successfully will be the most probable behavior that we will engage in at the present time. This is the principle of reinforcement, which we will discuss below.

Key Features of Behavior

Consistency

Behaviors are consistent. That is, if we have been able to solve our problem (deficit state) before by engaging in a certain behavior, we will tend to solve that problem in the same way again each time that it arises. This is what makes behaviors predictable. We do not try to reinvent the wheel each time we experience a need. We simply do the same thing we did before that effectively dealt with that problem. Granted, there are variations when it comes to specifics, but the general behavior is the same. For example, if we are hungry and crave meat, we will probably go to one of the places we know where we have had good meat in the past. Although we may have two or three places that we could go to, the general behavior of going to some place where we previously had a positive experience stands. This is not to say that time constraints and other factors won't enter into the equation, but the general tendency will depend on previous reinforcing experiences associated with the need in question.

This aspect of behavior lies on a continuum that ranges from good to bad. It is good when it saves time, gets you what you need and expect from the experience, and allows you to take care of other things that may be more pressing in your life. But you don't have to worry about where you will eat. On the other hand, it may exclude you from experiencing an even better new restaurant, and that restaurant may even be closer and would save you more time, and maybe save you money as well.

Addiction

Behaviors are habit forming or addictive. Given that all behavior is mediated through complex neurological, and therefore biochemical, reactions in the body, and the fact that we tend to engage in the same behavior over and over, our bodies get used to a certain consistent and repetitive pattern of biochemical stimulation. When such stimulation is not possible, we experience a degree of withdrawal similar to drug addiction, but not necessarily to the same intensity. Just ask any runner that sustains a sprained ankle and can't run for a few days how they feel. The degree of withdrawal will depend on the intensity of the stimulation and the length of time that the individual has been engaging in that behavior. The common phenomenon associated with this aspect of behavior is the old saying, "What's the matter with you? Did you get up on the wrong side of the bed this morning?" This is something that someone would say to a person who is not acting like his or her usual self. Although I cannot point to any experimental evidence to substantiate what I am about to say, I have directly experienced this phenomenon when my wife once fell asleep in my place. In an effort not to disrupt her sleep, I slept on the other side of the bed. In the morning, however, as I attempted to get out of bed, I noticed I was on the wrong side. This realization was enough to disrupt my regular routine, and in attempting to put my slippers on, I missed since it was not in the same place and required a different behavioral response. My responses became tenser as I attempted to complete my morning routine, resulting in putting me in a somewhat bad and irritable mood. Thus, what was a simple change in position resulted in a significant disruption in mood or emotion. I was very aware of this because I have always observed behavior, both my own as well as others'. So I am continuously questioning the motivation of my own behavior, and I find that it is rarely intentional and planned out but often dictated by the immediate environment and my emotional state. For example, I noticed that getting up in a strange place, such as a hotel, I also have to make behavioral responses that are not part of my usual morning routine. But the difference is that I am aware I am not home and things will be different. Thus, my internal expectation of what lies ahead has a great deal to do with my reaction. Thus, if I am expecting novelty and get novelty, I am not surprised. But if I expect sameness and get novelty, it disturbs the flow of behavioral responses that I think I should be making.

This rigid aspect of human behavior is responsible for a great deal more than just morning routines. In an effort to bring order into our world, we have solidified in our own experience "how things should be" and attempt to follow that flawed logic and get disappointed time after time. Having expectation through simple repetitive behavior can be fine when those expectations are confirmed by our experience. But inevitably, they will change, and we will be disappointed. The bus will not come on time, your dinner guests will not arrive just as soon as you have finished cooking their meals, and so on. The Chinese philosopher Lao Tzu said in the Tao Te Ching,

> A man is supple and weak when living, but hard and stiff when dead. Grass and trees are pliant and fragile when living, but dried and shriveled when dead. Thus the hard and the strong are the comrades of death; the supple and the weak are the comrades of life.

Thus, this addictive aspect of human behavior must be closely observed, and an effort made not to succumb to its easiness. We must acknowledge that sameness prevents new learning and disappointments are only the result of faulty expectations. If our expectations were always met, the world would be a static and uninteresting place. And indeed, in many ways, it does appear that the world is static. But if we observe closer, it is only in general terms that things are the same. In fact, each time we engage in the same behavior, it is always just a little bit different than the time before. Even if the behavior is as mundane as brushing our teeth or washing our hair. So although we like and gravitate toward sameness because it is easy, we must also welcome change as new ways to see and interact with the world around us. To achieve this, we must change our attitude about behaviors and their expectations. As Lao Tzu suggests, our attitude must be supple and weak. We must not cling to expectations as if they were reality. Only reality is reality. And it is not as neat or predictable as we envision it to be.

The neurophysiology of novelty and our experience of it are quite interesting and relevant in this discussion. It is well known that novelty gets our attention. It excites the brain because the brain does not have a previously established neural pattern of processing this information. Thus, the individual must process this new information by first becoming alert and aware of the differences as compared to previous experiences and make the adjustment. This is why in advertising, they keep selling us the same product, but it is constantly "new and improved." Simply stating this gets our attention because we want to know how it is new or improved. It gets our attention enough to hear the following statement that claims that it does what it used to do, but does it better.

Pribram (1971) states, "When monotonously stimulated, many neuronal aggregates show a decrementing of activity (adaption and habituation) and thus become sensitive to novelty (the orienting reaction)." He further states, "Amount of arousal is properly understood, therefore, as amount of match and mismatch between configurations, an amount of organization or disorganization, not an amount of excitation which is altered (see Hebb, 1949; Luria 1960). When the variety of perceptions exceeds to some considerable extent the repertory of action available to the organism, he feels 'interested' and is motivated to, i.e., attempts to extend this repertory."

One can see how reinforcing items quickly lose their effectiveness, primarily due to their sameness. Ironically, as discussed above, the addictive nature of behaviors aims to seek just that sameness because it requires little effort; and when that effort fails us, we become emotional. I should note that these two seemingly conflicting tendencies are not conflicting at all. They operate under different circumstances. Habituation occurs for the system to cope with situations that expose it to a stimulus repeatedly so that the individual can resume regular activity without constantly attempting to interpret and process this repetitive information. Novelty alerts the organism that something new has entered its space, which may be friendly or unfriendly, so that they can be on the lookout for what may be a right or wrong response in that particular situation, since by definition, the organism has not had any previous experience with the novel situation.

Ergonomic Soundness

Behaviors are motivated by cost-effective achievements of manipulating the environment. Another reason why behaviors are habit forming is simply due to their efficiency. We tend to accomplish tasks in the same way each time because it eliminates the time it takes to attempt to decide or figure out a new way of doing that which we already know how to do. This results in behavior that is cost-effective. As we shall see later, *ergonomics* plays a big role in the motivation of behavior. Simply stated, we want to alleviate discomfort, and we want to do it in the fastest and easiest way possible. The reason I state that behaviors are *usually* cost-effective is that this cost-effectiveness is dependent on our experience and education in reference to meeting whatever need is in question. With more experience and education, one can become more efficient or ergonomically correct in meeting their own needs (see the discussion on ergonomics below).

Again, this behavioral tendency, as all others, has a gradient of its own that spans from total laziness to hypervigilance. Laziness will inevitably leave much out of our behavioral response that could be of more benefit to us. But since you don't immediately see the effect of your laziness, it continues. For example, you may not brush your teeth as well as you should, but you won't get a cavity for a while. And by the time you do get a cavity, you may not necessarily link that with your laziness of how you brush. This may be brought to your attention by the dentist who proceeds to instruct you on how you should brush your teeth better to prevent further damage. The opposite is also true. For example, a hypervigilant person may brush their teeth so well that they actually damage their gum line. In this particular case, let me point out that this is a recurring theme in human behavior, as well as the human experience in general. Again, in Taoism, it is stated that

> hence constantly rid yourself of desires in order to observe its subtlety; but constantly allow yourself to have desires in order to observe what it is after.

Thus, the extremes on both ends can be detrimental to the individual, and moderation is the key.

Communicability

Behaviors are communicative in intent. No matter what the behavior is, one can analyze that behavior and come up with what the organism is stating about their condition at that moment. For example, if I am giving a lecture to a group of people and one person is falling asleep and is unresponsive to everything I am saying, that person is communicating their disinterest in what I am saying. If another is asking questions, is animated and engaged in the lecture, they are communicating that what I am saying is of some interest to them. Granted the reasons for both of these behaviors could be interpreted in many ways, the fact remains that one is communicating interest and the other, no interest. To see this process more clearly, watch one of those nature documentaries with the sound turned all the way down, and see if you can understand or comprehend what is being presented. Then turn the sound up and listen to see how the narrator is explaining it. This exercise will illustrate some tremendous variations on what is being communicated. Obviously, if you have had a lot of experience with the animals being portrayed, you are more likely to have a better grasp as to what the animal is "saying" or stating about their condition. This nonverbal assessment of communication is extremely important for reading emotional states, which I will discuss later. For the purpose of this discussion, I simply want to establish that behaviors are a communication of the organism's state and can be revealed to some degree through behavioral observation.

As with the other aspects of behavior, this one too has a gradient from being transparent to displaying a poker face. In some situations, you don't want to communicate your enthusiasm as, for example, when buying a car. You want to pretend you don't like the car that much and don't want to spend that much money on it. You want to communicate to the seller that you are not very motivated to buy it so that they will sweeten the deal, possibly by lowering the price. On the other hand, if you are attempting to gain employment in an interview, you want to communicate as much enthusiasm as possible concerning your desire to do a good job for the company.

One can characterize the communication problem as follows: individuals are an input/output biological organ that is constantly bombarded by stimuli or input. And we have three main outputs to respond to those inputs (see fig. 5). For example, let's say it is 7:00 AM and I go for a walk. The temperature is a little low, so I wear a sweater. Then by nine thirty, when the temperature gets much higher and I have been walking much longer, I begin to feel uncomfortable. Both internal and external inputs, or stimuli, are now motivating me to act differently to bring the level of discomfort down. My output options will consist of thinking about what to do (cognitive), get upset and angry at what is happening (emotional), or act on what is happening (behavioral). Furthermore, the individual can use a combination of those three, such as thinking about the best way to behave to get out of the situation or remedy the problem. The output channels in the illustration below go from clear to dark, implying that the clearest form of communication is actual behavior, while emotions and cognitive activity are not quite as effective in alleviating the environmental problem.

Stimulus Response Relationship

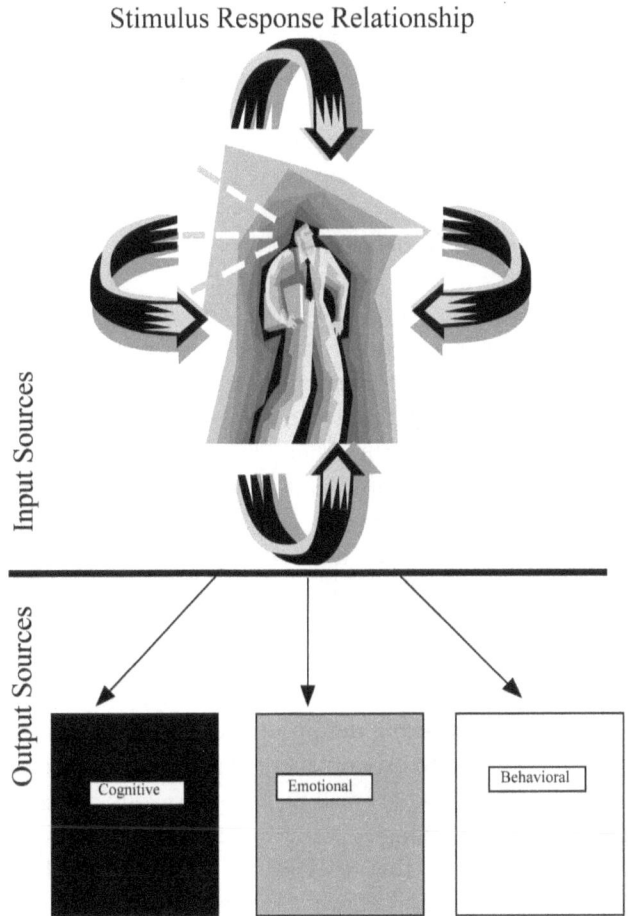

Input Sources

Output Sources

Cognitive

Emotional

Behavioral

Figure 5: Stimulus-response relations of
communication options

In working with the developmentally disabled, I try to impress
upon staff to communicate behaviorally since there are cognitive
deficits there that preclude fluid interaction, and emotions can
often be very confusing and puzzling. Thus, in communicating
with the low-functioning populations, one must keep words to a
minimum and behavioral demonstration to a maximum. I suggest
that this is the *main* difference between the developmentally
disabled population and the rest of us—the problem with

communication. As I said earlier, we have built a society that is highly dependent on verbal communication, and it is not the best form of expression when you want to get to the truth. That is why we have a lie detector test, so that we can listen to the body rather than the words that can easily be distorted, exaggerated, overstated or understated, depending on our need at the time.

Responsiveness and Reinforcement

Behaviors are the result of their consequences. They are responsive to environmental changes relative to themselves. Here, a discussion of reinforcement is relevant. For all behaviors are subject to manipulation through reinforcement, but the relationship, as with all of the other parameters mentioned, is not a linear or precisely predictable relationship. The general principle is simply that behaviors that are reinforced will increase in their future probability to occur. Those that are not will not increase and will eventually be extinguished as time passes and they are not reinforced. The difficulty with this simplistic relationship, although correct, does not explain or delve much in the understanding of what is reinforcement. There are various ways one can define reinforcement. The working definition I use is this: anything that an organism is willing to expend energy to obtain can be classified as a reinforcer. So if you are willing to spend your energy to get something, that something is a reinforcer for you. The problem with that definition is that it does not account for the cyclic pattern of needs described above, the satiation/deprivation cycle. For example, M&M'S may be reinforcing when used for the first few minutes of working with a child; but eventually, after eating a hundred or so M&M'S have been eaten by the child, they are no longer reinforcing. In fact, there is a predictable relationship between the amount of a reinforcer and its effectiveness, whereby the more of it you get, the less reinforcing it will become. Again, this relationship varies from person to person. Thus, when using reinforcers, it is best to use as many different items that are reinforcing as possible to prevent this satiation effect. Again, we see that the behavioral principles on which we rely that are objective, identifiable, and which we can be readily manipulated are dependent on the organism's internal state for their effectiveness and where in the gradient of needs they are at that moment. And this internal state cannot be directly observed, but its effects can indeed be measured and observed.

Another important feature of reinforcers is that they depend on internal need states. I would argue that the only things that are reinforcing are those things that fulfill the organism's needs in one way or another. This fulfillment is a biochemical and physiological process that is inherent in all biological organisms, including plants. In plant behavior, for example, the root systems will grow toward water and away from dry areas. In the same way, above the ground, the plant will lean toward the sun and thereby maximize its nutrition and chance for survival. Thus, organisms are predisposed to approach those things that make them feel better by meeting their needs, and tend to turn away from those things that harm them or don't do anything for them. Although we have not discovered every physiological mechanism responsible for indicating to our system that we are either satiated or deprived, we know that the hypothalamus is responsible for the regulation of many things such as hunger and satiation, thirst, heat, and other regulatory functions. As discussed in chapter 2, these regulatory sequences, when activated, will result in an internal state of discomfort. We become emotional. By experiencing these emotions, we become motivated to act. How we act and what guides this behavior will be the topic of the next few chapters. The general premise stands that behaviors are the result of their consequences depending on a variety of variables that come into play.

Usefulness

While many people may view inappropriate behaviors as maladaptive, I suggest that there is no such thing. Behaviors are always adaptive to some degree, and this is why they continue to be repeated. Behaviors that serve no purpose are usually abandoned for behaviors that do. So they may not be the most effective or best way to communicate needs or indicate some need, but they are always useful to the individual in their daily life and serve some kind of purpose for them. We shall see how this works when we discuss the *functional analysis* in the next chapter. By definition, a behavior that is never reinforced will eventually be extinguished since it serves no purpose. Even the severely mentally retarded population of developmentally disabled individuals can learn replacement behaviors and eventually give up inappropriate social behaviors (M. Cayem, University Microfilms International, 1986). Once the individual experiences and understands that it is in their best interest to behave differently, they will.

CHAPTER 6

The Functional Analysis

The mechanisms involved in studying behaviors in the classic behavioral approach will be covered in this chapter, as well as the not so classical. As many of you might know, behavioral psychologists do not evaluate problems by administering tests or measuring intellect by having the subject perform a series of tasks. The behavioral psychologist, or behaviorist, analyzes behaviors, one at a time, to find out what the functional relationship is between the behavior and its consequences. Thus, an individual may be exhibiting behavioral problems at home, at school, at a residential center, or at a day program. A behaviorist may be contacted by a variety of means or may be on the staff of that particular institution. If the problem occurs at home, the parents would usually contact the behaviorist either through a referral service or through the regional center system if the individual is a developmentally disabled person and is registered in the regional center system, the social services and case management agency that deals with the developmentally disabled. The job of the behaviorist is to assess the extent of the behavioral problem, find out what are the functional variables of which the behavior is the result, suggest a treatment plan, and train those in charge of the individual on how to do data collection and intervention of each of the problematic behaviors.

The process of any intervention begins with the *functional analysis*. The job of functional analysis is to assess what function is served by each of the target behaviors identified as reported by the individual or institution seeking the help. To find out, we look at what is called the ABCs of behavioral analysis: the antecedent, behavior, and consequence. In other words, we review the context of the behavior by analyzing its individual components, which I will discuss one at a time below.

The Antecedent

The antecedents can be anything that precedes the behavior and influences it in some way. What we are looking for is the particular antecedent that provoked the behavior so that in the planning of an intervention, we want to control or learn to deal with this provoking event. Antecedents could include settings such as malls, bowling alleys or concerts in the park, dinnertime, time to board the bus to go somewhere, or being in noisy environments. Antecedents can be physiological events such as internal pain, beginning the menstrual cycle, an ingrown toenail, a bowel obstruction, or a toothache. Antecedents can be emotional events, not only being happy or sad, but also more physiological emotions such as being hungry, anxious, or bored. Antecedents can be the time of day, such as early in the morning when certain people's processing power is low, or late in the day when the individual is tired and their coping skills are compromised. Antecedents can be the presence of particular people—people that one feels compelled to compete with, does not like in general, or someone the individual has had previous negative experiences with. Thus, antecedents can be emotional states that are aroused by certain individuals. Antecedents could include certain demands such as having to take a shower, wash the car, entertain guests, or doing homework.

Thus, we can see from the previous paragraphs that antecedents can be anything that has an impact on the individual in question and, specifically, on the behavior of the individual in question, namely, the behavior we are called to fix as behavior specialists. An antecedent is the stage onto which the behavior will be performed, the context of the behavior. As you can see in figure 6, which shows a simple tool for analyzing behaviors called the functional analysis chain chart, the antecedent may be nothing more than sitting in class. However, when one reviews this data later, it may be more than just sitting in class. When we look at the difference between the consequence for attending as opposed to disrupting, we see that the antecedent is sitting in class and *not* being attended to. Not being attended to results in an emotional state of boredom or disinterest in the teacher because of their presumed disinterest in the child. This is where I part with the purely behavioral variables. I assume boredom based on body language and reasoning from studying all of the other parameters of the behavior. It should be noted that I am oversimplifying this process for the purpose of illustration. In many cases, I have been wrong in conducting such an analysis because I did not observe long enough. For example, if I were to do this observation all day long, I may find out that Johnny only behaves this way during math. Further analysis may reveal that it is not, as we might assume, because he is not good at math but the contrary, that math is too easy for him and does not hold his attention. Hence the assumption that he is bored. Thus, it is very useful, when conducting this sort of observation, to interview people, even the subjects themselves, as to why they believe Johnny is acting this way. Some of the most useful information I have received in doing these observations came from the least knowledgeable people about behaviorism, the direct care staff. They knew the subject so well that they could predict and demonstrate what they were reporting to me. Thus, observation alone can reveal the function of the behavior, and you don't have to be very familiar with behaviorism to know this. You simply have to be a good observer. To complicate things further, it may not be a math class that is the problem but the teacher themselves. I found this out once when the student had two classes with this instructor and had behavioral problems only in those classes. One must come to the conclusion that emotionally, the teacher and the student are not compatible. Some teachers don't like certain students. That is a human fact. Ignoring this would be simply digging our head in the sand. In such a case, I urge that the two be separated. The child has the right to work with people that are able to get along with him. The teacher is getting paid to do a job, and they are unable to do it with this individual while others can. So why should the student be subjected to this sort of treatment? For the purpose of sticking to a schedule? What is the child learning? That the environment is a hostile one and cannot accommodate him? Does anyone believe the usual reason why we do this to children, which is to claim that the child needs to get along with all kinds of people and this would be good for them to be with someone they don't like? Personnel experience tells me that this is not the case. Teachers that have had a difficult time with me taught me nothing more than that school was stupid and teachers were stupid and that I was wasting my time there. As I mentioned earlier, I left home at fifteen, and escaping from having to go to school was a big part of my motivation to leave. Because no one took the time to analyze the antecedents to my behavior as I now get to do for others. I think this is why I wound up here doing this kind of work.

The Behavior

The behavior column (see fig. 6 below) must describe what the behavior is as accurately as possible. In this case, it is simply talking to a classmate, thereby disrupting the class. The behavior may not actually be that disruptive, but what constitutes a behavioral problem is in the eye of the beholder, the teacher, parent, or caretaker. And once the caretaker calls attention to the behavior, it is magnified, more disruptive, and very reinforcing to Johnny since his behavior produced such a significant environmental change. Controlling environmental effects is inherently reinforcing since our very survival depends on it. Thus, when we exhibit a behavior and immediately see a result in the environment, it is usually reinforcing, unless of course the consequences that follow are severe enough to override that reinforcement. In general, we behave to have an impact on our environment. Thus, when we see an immediate result in response to our behavior, that response, good or bad, will be reinforcing to some degree. But simply speaking, the behavior should describe what the person is doing. The actual act itself—talking to classmate while the lesson is being conducted. As you can see in figure 6, the behavior logged was "Johnny talks to classmate and disrupts class." This is *not* correct. Johnny simply talked to his classmate. Whether it is disruptive or not depends on the time that Johnny engaged in the behavior. So "disrupts class" should not be part of the description of the behavior. Instead, you could say he talked while a lesson was in session or while the teacher was talking, etc., because you may find that Johnny only talks when the teacher spends a lot of time writing something on the board and Johnny gets bored while waiting, then starts to talk until the teacher is finished. Thus, Johnny's behavior is an emotional reaction. A behavior plan to reduce that behavior would be different than one that consists of talking and interrupting the teacher while they are talking or only when they are talking. That would be a more severe and more disruptive form of talking in class.

In summary, as I attempted to illustrate in the above paragraph, you must be clear about the behavior you are describing and don't assume anything because the slightest difference will provoke a behavioral plan that may not fit the situation. The behavior targeted must be described accurately and without adjectives. We certainly don't want Johnny to stop talking altogether. And neither do we want Johnny to stop talking in class. The hope is that Johnny can learn when and when not to talk. But this again is an assumption we make. Johnny probably knows when to talk and not talk, but Johnny cannot contain himself when bored. So Johnny will need to learn a completely different skill, one of self-control or redirection to an activity that is not disruptive to the teacher.

The Consequence

The consequence of any behavior must be described from the point of view of the one engaging in the problematic behavior. In other words, in the example below, the consequence would *not* be that the instructor disapproved of Johnny's behavior or that he or she gave Johnny a stern look signaling that they did not like what he did, because these behaviors describe what the teacher is doing and *not* what Johnny is experiencing as a result of his behavior. Receiving attention from the teacher and all of the students in the class *is* the consequence for Johnny and not any of those other things going on around him. It is what is happening to him that is the issue.

Antecedent	Behavior	Consequence
Johnny in class.	Johnny attending to lesson in class.	Nothing
Johnny in class.	Johnny attending to lesson in class.	Nothing
Johnny in class.	Johnny talks to classmate and disrupts class.	Teacher and students pay attention to Johnny.

Figure 6: A functional analysis chain chart

What the behavioral scientist must do to arrive at a workable analysis of the behavior in question is a direct observation of the individual exhibiting the inappropriate behavior and simply documenting what is happening before, during, and after the behavior to detect a pattern in the occurrence of the problematic behavior. In general, what we usually observe is a pattern of an antecedent that is unpleasant to the individual, followed by an inappropriate behavior, and that behavior results in a change in the environmental parameters that provoked the behavior. So staying with the same example, what we can conclude is that Johnny likes attention since he engages in this behavior a lot, according to the teacher, and here he was doing what he is supposed to do, namely, attending to the lesson in class. But doing so does not produce what he likes, which is attention from others. Thus, an uneasiness arises that provokes a behavioral response to alleviate this discomfort, and this behavior is usually something he has engaged in previously that produced the desired result—attention.

A strict behaviorist would object to my use of the terms *likes, uneasiness,* and *discomfort,* all of which are emotional parameters inside the individual that do not fit the strictly objective behavioral approach. The purist would argue that we don't know that any of those things are actually occurring, and thus we cannot use such terminology in a functional analysis of behaviors. The behaviorist would prefer to describe the behavior in objective terms. So Johnny does not "like" anything; he merely cannot tolerate not being attended to for long periods. When he is in a situation that demands that, he engages in escape behavior that results in getting attention. I find such characterizations to be at odds with human experience and not quite accurate. People don't just evolve into individuals who cannot tolerate the lack of attention. This intolerance occurs for a reason. It could be lack of attention at home, so Johnny must seek it out at school, or it may be that he simply does not like the teacher and is engaging in the behavior to irritate him or her, or a host of other reasons. But the fact remains that the motivation to act in such a way is unique to that individual, since most of the other students are not behaving in the same way. This uniqueness points to something inherent in the individual that is engaging in the behavior, and *not* to something having to do with the topography of the situation, since all of the other students are subjected to the same environmental topography. Behaviorists would simply point to reinforcement history. I would argue that this something that is provoking the behavior is *not* solely an environmental event. Two reasons come to mind here. First, if it was strictly the environment, then many students would react in this way, and usually, this is not the case. The other more relevant observation is that Johnny does not *always* exhibit the behavior in question, but only once in a while. Obviously, he engages in the behavior frequently enough to be referred for special attention, which appears to be what he wants. If we continue on with this logic, intervention then becomes just more reinforcement for Johnny since he is getting more attention by having people formally targeting his behavior. Rather than Johnny learning not to engage in the behavior, Johnny learns that engaging in the behavior produces even more attention. Indeed, I have seen many cases where this chain of events occurs and the behavior gets worse, not due to the well-known extinction burst (see "Extinction Burst" below) that occurs as a result of instituting most intervention plans since they interfere with the individual's previous coping behavioral skills, but, rather, due to the increased attention focused on the behavior. Let me point out that this chain of events is not the norm but does occur frequently enough to require special attention.

77

The point here is to not interfere with behaviors unless it is absolutely necessary. Because of the scenario described above, intervention should attempt to ignore the inappropriate behaviors while focusing on building new behaviors that accomplish the same result for the person exhibiting the behavior. This is usually called *building replacement behaviors* and rests on the assumption that the individual exhibiting the behavior is being reinforced for it in some way, and so we aim to find a more appropriate way for them to gain that reinforcement. Emotionally, the individual *needs*, *wants*, and *likes* the results of their behavior because they continue to repeat it. So the trick is to teach them a more appropriate way of getting that result. Put in behavioral sociobiological terms, the behavior meets some need, and needs do not go away with punishment or lack of reinforcement. So we teach the individual to meet that need in a more appropriate way with a replacement behavior that is socially acceptable.

The Use of Subjective Data in a Functional Analysis

As I proposed in earlier chapters, I believe in and have used subjective variables to guide my understanding of inappropriate behaviors and have successfully used such data in the development of effective intervention techniques. A few examples will serve to illustrate how this can be done.

I had a patient once who was quite aggressive in his response to not getting what he wanted or when changes were introduced that did not agree with him or when changes to his daily routine were implemented that he was not adequately prepared for. This individual was developmentally disabled and moderately mentally retarded. Due to his explosive and aggressive reactions, the people in charge of his care would frequently give in to whatever he wanted, thus exacerbating the problem. It was my job to fix this problem. After doing my functional analysis and reinforcement survey (see Reinforcement Survey in the appendix) to determine what he might respond to, I settled on a behavioral contract (see Behavioral Contract in the appendix) that required the absence of any episodes of physical aggression for a month to earn a lunch out with me to any place he wanted and eat whatever he wanted. Those two things, going out with me and eating out at a restaurant for lunch, were very high on his list of reinforcers. The program was not very successful. Out of six months on this program, he had earned this lunch only twice. Then on a day that I was working at the day program site that he was attending, I heard some commotion in the other room. I quickly ran out to see what was going on, and there he was, physically fighting with another client. I immediately intervened and physically separated them. I had a staff take the other client away from the area, and I escorted the client I am talking about to my office. I remember being very frustrated with him and began talking to him as if I was talking to a friend in a frustrated and almost-angry tone—something I rarely do with clients. I simply asked him what the heck he was doing, striking out at this person when he was due to go out to lunch with me the following week. He simply said, "Revenge." I repeated the word to make sure I understood, and he nodded affirmatively. So I asked him why he wanted revenge and for what. He reported that this person spat at him, and he pointed to the back of his head. Sure enough, there was a disgusting mass of mucus still there. So I explained to him that this was not really getting revenge since he was the one that lost out on the outing with me, and even though the other individual also lost the outing for that day, so did he; so he lost both the outing and lunch as a result of his poor self-control. So I suggested to him that if he really wanted to get revenge, he should have immediately reported the incident to me or to another staff member, and I assured him that it would have been the offender and not him, who would have lost the outing. So he can then inform the other individual of this result and report to him the good time he had on the outing that the offender was not able to go to. Although I had never suggested such a plan, and haven't since, it seemed a good idea at the time. I was desperately searching for an appropriate replacement behavior for him to engage in other than striking out at others, and this seemed like an appropriate response. Within a matter of a few months, this individual graduated out of the behavioral program and began earning money at a sheltered workshop, where he never had another assaultive episode. But he became a big tattle-tale, reporting the infractions of others frequently to get them in trouble and get attention for himself as well!

In the example just described, I had been diligent in implementing a functional analysis and had known that provocation by others was a factor in his assault, but I could find no appropriate way of getting this client to understand the importance of engaging in the replacement behavior. Teaching clients to report infractions to staff instead of attempting to deal with them on their own, especially if they have a tendency to be aggressive, is a standard behavior plan in day programs such as the one I am describing. However, when this particular client would do this, staff would assure him that they would take care of the problem and have the client go and apologize to him, have them shake hands, and then consider the matter resolved. This was not satisfactory to the client I am referring to, and he wanted more in line with his feelings of the need for revenge. Thus, it was a matter of convincing him that what I was suggesting was real revenge, and that if he were smart, he would engage in the replacement behavior instead of striking out at the other person. This is an illustration of using subjective data, reported by the person having the problem, to develop and implement an effective behavior plan. The only real intervention here was to change his attitude about the problem. To make him believe that what I was suggesting was real revenge and what he was doing was getting him in trouble. In this example, I am in no way suggesting that behavioral plans should be abandoned for this approach. On the contrary, I continued with the behavioral contract, and it was much more successful with the additional verbal mediation dealing with his feelings. Perception is everything! I should also mention that this is a person who was trained to express his feelings and felt entitled to have his feelings addressed. So the only thing I did was work with what I had.

In another case, a female client lost her mother to cancer and was extremely lonely and sad. This lady was severely retarded and functionally nonverbal, although she could communicate with gestures quite well. Staff did what they could to soothe her; I talked with her about her mother and acknowledged that she probably missed her and that was OK, etc., as we would do with cases such as these. However, this particular client went into a deep depression, and psychotropic medications were required to help her cope with the situation. The medication was somewhat effective in reducing her self-isolation and getting her to the day program on a daily basis, but she was not her usual self being very friendly and social. Again, the turnaround event for her, as with the one mentioned in the introduction, was when a staff person took her on as her surrogate mother. Frankly, I do not condone such relationships because oftentimes the client will develop a strong attachment, but then the person they look to for emotional support finds another job and forgets all about them, thus provoking another episode of depression.

Although there are environmental measures that I have used effectively in the past to deal with depression, nothing seems to be as potent as a significant emotional bond and relationship with another human being. The individual simply needs a friend. We can claim that this is not scientific, and we would be correct; but again, I would like to focus the readers' attention to the whole point of applied behavioral analysis, which is the practical control of problematic behavior, and the development of more appropriate prosocial, and—I would add—proemotional, behaviors. It is this last point that I would like to elaborate on more fully since it is completely ignored in most behavioral literature because it is deemed unsuitable. I would argue that it is very suitable in practice, and adding this dimension to the practice of applied behavioral analysis takes nothing away from it, but, rather, adds something to it. This addition is the dimension of emotion, which is part of the individual's internal environment. Thus, we are attempting to utilize the individual's internal environment to change behavior. Developing ways to detect and respond to the behavioral signs of internal states would be a fruitful find for the behavior analyst and could provide a deeper understanding of the problem. Let me repeat, the word *applied* in applied behavior analysis implies the *practice* of the science in the natural world. And the natural world has so many variables that we cannot control that we are always working in the realm of approximations. Applied behavior analysis is based on scientific principles. However, when those principles are applied in the natural world, they come into contact with variables that the analyst knows are there but chooses to ignore because they cannot be measured. But can any behavior analyst claim that these emotions have no bearing on behavior whatsoever? And if so, what evidence is there to demonstrate this belief?

Communication Is the Key

In general, we have built a society that operates under the assumption that we can all communicate using words and speech patterns learned early in life. However, many people miss the other signals of communication that are much more relevant than the words that are spoken. Those other cues are actually more accurate than the spoken words that are very much influenced by popular culture and social mores. Thus, although you may want to curse at your boss for being so stupid, you will not do so because it would be considered inappropriate and you may lose your job. However, when your boss is being stupid, you may make a certain face, cringe, or be unusually silent in response to their behavior. These nonverbal cues are much more honest and automatic and less colored by popular culture. Speech, or verbal communication in general, has rules and is highly structured. It is precisely the absence of such rules in the emotional expression of experience that makes it a more reliable measure of the individual's internal state. I would argue that all inappropriate behaviors are simply inappropriate ways of communicating needs.

In working with the developmentally disabled or handicapped population who are unable to speak, it becomes necessary for the individual to learn sign language or to make gestures that can communicate those needs effectively to others. When needs arise, as they inevitably do, the individual has only two options. The first option is to act on the need with a behavior that will meet that need. When such a response is not possible due to the person's handicap, the individual is forced to rely on speech, sign language, or the use of gestures to communicate their need. When all of those options are not available due to profound handicaps of speech or intellectual level, it is incumbent on the caretaker to read the individual's need based strictly on facial expressions and behavior.

In those cases where the individual is not able to communicate with speech, sign language, or consistent or purposeful facial expression, the caretaker should pay special attention to physiological needs. For example, the caretaker must keep track of when was the last time the individual got to go to the bathroom, the last time they had a drink, the last time they had something to eat, if they are appropriately dressed for the current weather conditions so that they are not too cold or hot. Those physiological needs are obvious because we all experience them and all of us have to attend to them. Thus, we have to assume a similar schedule of needs in the individuals whose care we are responsible for. This may or may not be the case for that particular individual; but with close observation of behavioral patterns, facial expression, etc., we are able to get to know how the individual reacts when hungry, thirsty, or uncomfortable. In many cases, what the individual will experience are things that cannot be interpreted. This may include the experience of boredom, the need to be left alone, or the need to simply be talked to, acknowledged, or receive affection from others to meet their social needs. Although we are not able to see any of these needs behaviorally, we may be able to guess as to what they may be based on the individual's past history and reaction to others who deal with them. For example, we may note that the individual is more active in the mornings and therefore can engage in more behaviors and participate in more activities at that time. Or we can observe that they are sluggish in the morning and come to life in the afternoon. Thus, we should schedule programming or activities at that time instead. The idea is that no matter how debilitated, there is still an exchange that could be characterized as communication. What we are attempting to do is to anticipate the need of the individual and meet that need on a schedule that is based on our observation of the individual's behavior—behavior that is communicated through subtle physiological responses, no matter how minute those responses may be. The important point here is that in those cases of severe and extreme debilitation of the usual behavioral responses, including the ability to speak, we come to understand that behaviors are provoked from internal biochemical physiological deficit states that require attention. Thus, the lack of expressive speech and the presence of needs are important antecedents to the functional analysis, which may be missed since they are not directly observed.

The Need for Attention

Too often I hear from staff, teachers, and parents that the individual exhibiting behavioral problems is simply doing this for attention, implying that the need for attention is not a legitimate need, nor is it indicative of a deeper, more relevant need such as, perhaps, discomfort. The other implication that is often made is that because they are exhibiting the behavior for attention, then giving them attention will simply reinforce the inappropriate behavior, and this attention should be withheld instead of given. Although I would agree that attention should not be provided in response to inappropriate behavior, I would argue that attention, even if it is not indicative of some deeper underlying need, is an essential need, every bit as important as eating, drinking, and sleeping. Caspar Whitney in "The View-Point" (Seven Days' Book, *the OUTING Magazine*, vol. L [April–September 1907], 749) said "that it is more lucrative to be damned than to be ignored," meaning that an individual would rather you disapprove of their way of seeking attention but get that attention nevertheless.

One of my professors in applied behavior analysis once said that the only known universal reinforcers are sweets and attention. Both can be used to shape behavior in many animals. Attention is a necessary requirement of the individual, and so is touch. John Bowlby (February 26, 1907, to September 2, 1990) studied World War II infants who died in orphanages despite being fed and changed. The high rate of mortality was found to result from the babies not being cuddled. Once they instituted cuddling sessions throughout the day, the mortality rate decreased. Dr. Bowlby was a British psychiatrist and psychoanalyst, known for his work in child development and attachment theory. Dr. Bowlby advanced the idea that attachment behavior was essentially an evolutionary survival strategy for protecting the infant from predators. He showed that attachment security at fifteen and twenty-four months predicts aggressive behavior at fifty-four months (*Developmental* Psychology 28 [1992], 759–775).

The work of Dr. Bowlby and others spurred much experimental work in the years that followed that led to the famous Harlow experiments with monkeys, which studied the effects of affection, love, and separation from the mother. Harlow's conclusion was as follows:

> From the developmental point of view, the general plan is quite clear: The initial love responses of the human being are those made by the infant to the mother or some mother surrogate. From this intimate

attachment of the child to the mother, multiple learned and generalized affectional responses are formed. (Harry F. Harlow, *The Nature of Love* [University of Wisconsin, first published in *American Psychologist*, vol. 13, 1958], 673–685)

The research, although not conclusive, points to love and affection as actual and real needs in individuals. Remembering the gradient effect from the earlier chapters, one can see that attention would be the low end of affection, or love and sexual intercourse would be at the high end of the need for affection. One must get noticed to curry favor and eventually become loved. Harlow's research showed a relationship between the lack of affection, as defined by contact with a mother, and disturbances in development. It appears that a certain amount of affection as defined behaviorally by close physical contact of a nurturing kind is essential for normal growth. You would think that this would be a self-evident observation. But in the scientific realm, everything must be proven or demonstrated to be a viable and objective parameter.

Attention is particularly important for the handicapped. Due to their inability to function properly as a result of their disability, there are many situations in which they are unable to get what they need without assistance. Thus, learning ways of attracting attention is an extremely useful tool. In many situations, a developmentally disabled individual is seeking attention not just to get attention but to alert you to one of their needs such as needing to be assisted to get to the restroom or get a drink of water. Once staff understand the pattern and respond appropriately, they reinforce the inappropriate behavior because it succeeded in bringing about a change in you, the interventionists, instead of bringing about a change in them, the ones with the inappropriate behavior. Again, communication is the key, and this should be the primary focus of all interventions—more effective communication skills to express needs and preferences.

Sensory Deprivation

Another antecedent that is not readily observed is that of sensory stimulation/deprivation. In particular, individuals with developmental disabilities are often sensory deprived due to a disruption in the reciprocity of their ability to respond to affection. By this I mean that due to their lack of responsiveness or slowness of responding to affection, the mother is not immediately reinforced for her behaviors of affection toward the child. Thus, the amount of affection-type behaviors exhibited by the mother may not be as frequent as those in a normal relationship of mother and child. Often, family members don't know what to do with this child who does not act normal; and usually the mother, as well as other family members, will develop a relationship of accommodation with the child. Attention is provided only when certain needs must be met. But the general playful and social interactions are not as frequent. Family members actually tend to do the opposite of what should be done, namely, to stimulate the child more and subject them to different forms of stimulation since they tend to be less curious than normal children who are constantly seeking out stimulation on their own. That stimulation must be introduced to them. This is largely a communication problem. The child is unable to communicate with the mother in the normal way. It is up to the environment to remedy this situation through interaction and stimulation on a more intensive level than would be done with a normal child. When this is not done, the child often begins to exhibit self-injurious behaviors that are self-stimulatory in nature, but can increase in intensity to cause actual physical injury. The degree of intensity will depend on the degree and intensity of stimulus deprivation. The danger here is that as the child acclimates to the self-stimulatory behavior and it becomes routine, they tend to increase the intensity of the stimulation to expose themselves to new stimulation. Thus, an increase in intensity replaces variety for the child who is unable to be more creative in seeking stimulation. And as the years go by and this process is repeated over and over, what looked like self-stimulation now looks like self-injurious behavior. We know from infant-stimulation programs that stimulation does facilitate learning and the receptivity of the child to respond to those things around them.

There's been much focus on stimulation programs in recent years, usually from the field of occupational therapy, as well as from recreational therapy consultants. These consultants evaluate the person; and if they engage in self-injurious behavior, they are placed on a sensory diet, where staff stimulate them for five or ten minutes at a time, two or three times a day. An example of such stimulation may consist of using brushes that are applied to the arms, weighted blankets, swing chairs, etc., to introduce the individual to a variety of sensations that are not normally encountered in everyday life. This practice has become so popular that many day programs have "sensory rooms" with disco lighting, swing chairs, brushes, and textured items for them to feel. There appears to be a correlation between receiving sensory stimulation and a reduction in self-injurious behaviors.

In summary, what is being suggested here is that in addition to implementing the functional analysis of the behavior in relation to the immediate environment, it is useful to keep in mind the communicable ability of the individual, their history of sensory stimulation, and the quality of their relationship with family members relative to being touched, hugged, and whether they are included in all aspects of family functions. These parameters can contribute much to the level of intensity and frequency of behaviors observed. In general, it has been my experience that the more deprived of sensory stimulation the individual is, the more intense the behaviors that seek that stimulation. However, this is dependent on the general level of need of the individual in question. For example, hyperactive children require more stimulation than those who are not. Again, all individuals are unique in their histories and needs, and this is just a general statement concerning the input and output channels alluded to earlier concerning communication flow. Individuals are constantly seeking that balance that is comfortable for them, whether they are disabled or normal, human or other animal. The biological tendencies are the same throughout but expressed differently in each specie. When the individuals are impaired in some way and unable to seek and find that balance, it is up to the caretakers to evaluate and attempt to provide that balance whenever possible. Thus, in addition to having behavioral plans for specific behaviors, the general plan is to help the individual maintain a balance. A balance means meeting needs. When needs are met, the organism is at rest. There is no anxiety. There is no depression. Both are perceptual problems, which believe that their needs are not met, or will not be met. The depressed person feels that their needs are not met and may never be met, and the anxious person is afraid that their future needs will not be met. The function of much behavior that results from this type of situation is unproductive because it operates under a false premise. This is where cognition becomes essential in understanding behavior. The anxious person believes that catastrophe can happen at any moment and probably will. The depressed person believes that there is no point in finding happiness, because if it hasn't been found up until now, it probably will never be found for them. In both cases, a shift in cognitive thinking is required for real progress to come about. An attitude shift sparked by cognitive restructuring.

CHAPTER 7

Emotions: The Fuel That Provokes Behavior

Before I delve into the topic of emotions, let me state that I am very well aware of the lack of evidence or proof for anything I am stating in this chapter, but I view this chapter as the key to my entire thesis of this discussion on applied behavior analysis—that subjective and nonquantifiable variables *can* effectively be used in a functional analysis. These internal and private events that are accessible only to the individual experiencing them are probably the most powerful parameters determining how one will behave. Biological entities are a mass of living tissue that expands and contracts, opens and closes, blocks or facilitates biochemical traffic throughout the entire organic unit—the individual. This organic unit responds to these internal events, and these responses are shaped by the immediate environment in which they find themselves. Thus, the internal imbalance or need of the organism results in an emotional state that creates the motivation that will evoke behaviors. What behavior will be exhibited and how the need will be expressed will depend completely on the environment and the opportunities it offers, as well as the individual's reinforcement history in relation to that environment.

If the individual is not adept at manipulating the environment effectively to meet their needs, they will likely attempt to communicate their need in other ways. Usually, they will exhibit behaviors that do not help them restore the balance they are seeking. More accurately, the individual is compelled to seek, and the need becomes more pressing and the behaviors, no matter what they are, become more intense as the need intensifies in time. As I attempted to illustrate in figure 3, deficit states (translated to

89

the individual as emotional states of discomfort) and motivational states work hand in hand in such a way that as the organism fails to meet their deficit state, their motivational state increases, and the organism starts going through their repertoire of responses in an attempt to meet their immediate need. Continued failure will produce more intense emotional reactions due to biochemical mechanisms that continue to throw the organism more out of balance until the organism's response repertoire is depleted and they resort to severe behavioral reactions that are surely to get the attention of those around them. And hopefully, those people around them may do something for them that will alleviate their pressing need.

I have observed this pattern many times; and since the consequences of such behaviors have often been detrimental to me, personally, my motivation to solve this problem was quite high, especially when I was in a small classroom with ten developmentally disabled students, four of whom could become physically aggressive, seemingly for no reason. Careful observation would prove otherwise. There is always a reason for the outburst; but because we, the observers, do not observe well and fail to take steps to alleviate the discomfort that the person in our care is experiencing, we suffer the consequences and wonder why in the world the students react in this manner. Thus, it became my project to find out why to prevent any further attacks on my person. It is due to these experiences that I shifted more to internal events rather than remain totally focused on the environment, which was my training and experience in applied behavior analysis. I needed a way to deal with these internal states. Behaviorism had little to offer in this area, and psychodynamic theories were of little use. Furthermore, I did not and could not abandon the behavioral approach since I had done much experimental work in the laboratories of CSULA (California State University, Los Angeles), worked with severely handicapped populations, and knew empirically the power and soundness of the behavioral approach. But this part of the puzzle was not solved for me. So I set out to structurally observe the behavioral correlates of emotions since there was much experiential data I could draw from, but nothing in a way I could use to further my effectiveness as a behaviorist. The following are some guidelines as to how one can utilize and respond to emotional cues and, more importantly, to be able to use that information in a behavioral approach to solve problem behaviors. As I have hinted above, this line of thinking has been fruitful and effective in dealing with behavioral issues when a strictly environmental functional analysis was not enough.

Emotions

When I talk about the use of nonquantifiable data within the context of a functional analysis, what I am primarily talking about is emotions. These pesky feelings that make us uncomfortable, make us feel good, make us listless and apathetic, make us motivated or happily unproductive. Emotions are the playground of politicians and advertising firms. In both of these fields, the use of words in combination with images is used to change behavior. Unfortunately, the change in behavior in question is geared to benefit the person using those words and images, usually to vote for them or buy their product. In short, their aim is to get you to believe in what they are portraying with these words and images. They do this by appealing to your natural human emotions that we all experience. For them, they don't need to argue about whether emotions are scientific, objective, or measurable. For them, the results speak for themselves. If the product sells, the campaign continues. If the people vote for them, the campaign continues. Results are the main focus, as behavior change should be the main focus for applied behavioral analysis.

The group of natural human emotions used, as I see it, is quite small in number. Usually, it consists of appealing to one's sexuality, safety, social acceptance, or hedonistic drive to feel good. Not a long list. In fact, one can further reduce it to simply hedonistic aspirations since sex, safety, and social acceptance all make us feel good. The reason why manipulation is possible through these means is because we all want to feel good. Feeling good is simply the complete absence of not feeling good. Since all humans share a similar genetic structure, they also share a similar set of biological needs. The Dalai Lama writes,

> The basic thing is that everyone wants happiness, no one wants suffering. And happiness mainly comes from

our own attitude, rather than from external factors. If
your own mental attitude is correct, even if you remain
in a hostile atmosphere, you feel happy.

And the job of the advertiser, salesman, or politician is to
convince you that if you do what they tell you, you will be happy.
Of course, these are usually false premises, and most people, even if
they succumb to the call to behave in this particular manner, do not
actually feel good or happy. They may think they feel better because
they are doing something that many others are doing, thus creating
the illusion that they are part of a cohesive group. But in reality, if
those people are usually irritable and unhappy, they will continue to
be irritable and unhappy after voting or buying whatever it is they
were convinced to do. These acts do not fundamentally change
anything in their lives. The only thing that will actually change
your life is changing your attitude. As I attempted to illustrate
in the last chapter, a change in the attitude of the person who
wanted revenge was all that was needed to change his behavior.
This attitude was changed through verbal mediation alone. No
reinforcers, no consequences, and no contractual agreement. This
is something that is largely ignored in behavior therapy but is given
some consideration in cognitive behavior therapy. In fact, it is the
main objective in psychodynamic therapy as well as in many other
forms of "talking" therapies. The assumption is that awareness and
understanding will result in a change in attitude, which will then
translate into a change in behavior on its own. I would argue that
both are necessary for real behavior change, and I view behavior
change not simply as engaging in a different response class but as
actually responding to the same stimuli from a different perspective
or understanding, thus resulting in a change in behavior. What I
am referring to here is a *perceptual change* in how one views and
understands the antecedent to their inappropriate behavior. For
example, in the story of the vengeful client mentioned above, the
antecedent for aggressive behavior is usually a change or provocation
by another client that was the signal for revenge, and revenge was
viewed as striking out at the provoking agent. These antecedents
gave rise to emotions interpreted by the subject as being disrespectful
of his feelings. However, with the new perception of viewing this
provocation as an opportunity to get them in trouble by reporting

them while saving oneself from getting in trouble with them, the old behavior disappears and the replacement behavior takes hold. This new replacement behavior results in the client feeling better about the negative episode because it was successfully handled. He gets reinforced for his appropriate behavior, and he observes that the other client gets punished, so his feelings of revenge are satisfied. The change is largely a perceptual one that has behavioral correlates such as a change in *attitude*.

I had another patient that was very high functioning, within the mild range of mental retardation that could not speak at all, but was very adept at making his needs and preferences known to others. This individual would occasionally have temper tantrums where he would yell, scream, slam and break things in his room, usually his own, and would isolate himself until he calmed down. This is a person who was a foreman on a gardening crew at a supported employment program. While I don't have any evidence to support what I am about to say, I have simply observed that the higher-functioning developmentally disabled individuals are much more aware of their retardation and demonstrate a much higher need to prove their "rank" among the lower-functioning individuals, thus engaging in various behaviors such as bossing others, correcting others, and being quick to tell instructors, "I know, I know!" As a result, they are also very sensitive to criticism. In doing the functional analysis of this individual to determine the function of his temper tantrums, it was clear that he engaged in this behavior when one of two things happened:

1. He was required to make a verbal response in front of others
2. When he was asked to do something that he tried but failed to do

In both cases, it turns out, he was made to look retarded in front of an audience. While he was very capable of nodding yes and no in public, he could not handle having to communicate in front of a group of normal people when yes and no were not an option. It turns out that he would get embarrassed, and his only way out is to engage in his temper tantrum behavior, which was always successful in helping him escape the necessity to try and communicate and, in the process, look stupid in front of others.

Having discovered this chain of events in doing the functional analysis, the behavior plan was simple: when out in public and in need of a response from him, ask him only questions that he can answer with yes or no responses. If more was required, staff simply needed to take him to a private area and talk to him alone. This simple behavior plan has been successful 100 percent of the time when implemented in the manner described, but only in references to verbal utterances. However, if you will recall what I stated earlier, another antecedent is assigning him a task that he cannot successfully complete. In that case, staff was instructed to not ever ask him to do anything that he could possibly fail at, but simply ask him to help you do it so that staff can pick up where he leaves off or where they see he is having trouble. This prevents the escalation and avoids making him responsible for being a failure, yet another emotion that provokes the behavior.

The use of emotions in a functional analysis that attempts to deal with inappropriate behaviors does *not* abandon the behavioral approach but, rather, facilitates its success by focusing on relevant variables of the individual experiencing them, although those variables remain private. Although I was trained in the science of behaviorism, when I am confronted with behavioral problems in various social settings such as schools, day programs, or residential centers, I am very aware of the limitations of those environments and what can be achieved in those settings. I would argue that a purely scientific treatment of behavioral issues in those environments is practically impossible. We are always working with approximations. There are too many variables that cannot be controlled, such as staff stability, level of training of staff, compatibility issues, consistency issues, and disruptions due to home visits, holidays, deaths in the family, and so on. And these are only the common ones that we deal with on a daily basis. The point here is that we behaviorists often do not have the luxury of implementing a clean and scientific behavior program with reliability measures, accurate data collection, or even consistent implementation of the plan. So I am forever attempting to form and shape staff attitudes toward the individual in question or the population as a whole. I have found that individual behavior plans are best understood within the context of a global view of the person or population at large. This view is one that explains human behavior on an experiential level. We all experience emotions. So appealing to those emotions and putting them within the context of behavioral problems result in staff understanding the need and logic for the behavior plan. Thus, instead of viewing the client as someone who is uncooperative and acting out, they come to view a person with needs that cannot be communicated and thus left to wallow in their state of discomfort and pain with no way out. They are prisoners within their own bodies, just like the rest of us.

Pain and Aversive Emotion

Another dimension of emotions that we don't see discussed or dealt with is that of the visibility of emotions. Again, this is not a parameter that can be verified or proven; but hopefully, you will come to understand my logic once my reasoning is carefully described. Simply stated, I believe that developmentally disabled individuals, especially the nonverbal ones, believe that we can see their pain, literally. I came to this conclusion after years of experience in the field, and I will describe how I arrived at such a conclusion.

Whenever one of my patients has a difficult time and staff is unable to control them, they usually call me and ask for advice. The most unusual cases are those of patients I have seen many times and who don't normally have significant behavioral issues. Then all of a sudden, they are extremely agitated and assaultive. To complicate matters, they go after and beat up on their favorite staff, usually the home manager or live-in staff that is there all the time. What is unusual is the person they target. Why would they want to hurt those who care for them the most? On my first such case, I was baffled, called the psychiatric emergency team (PET), and facilitated a hospitalization. Eventually, the hospital staff finds some ailment that is quite painful, such as an impacted tooth requiring extraction or bowel obstruction; and once they fix the problem, the patient returns home with no further behavioral episodes of assault.

On one particular morning, I myself was suffering from a severe toothache, the kind that pounds and pulsates on the side of my face. The pain was so severe that I actually thought the pulsations would be visible to the naked eye. So I went to the mirror and looked closely at that area with no evidence of anything that could be seen with the naked eye even though I could still feel it pulsate. That morning, I was on my way to investigate just such a case as the one I described, where the patient was beating up on their favorite staff although they had never assaulted others previously. Immediately, I could see why they were assaultive and why they were assaulting their favorite staff. My logic is this: if anyone should be empathetic to my needs, as a developmentally disabled person who is under your care, it is those that are the closest to me and in charge of my care. So if I am in pain and it continues to get worse and worse and my care provider does not care enough to do anything for me, my pain eventually becomes unbearable. A functional analysis would reveal that the assaults are a function of the pain and the lack of alleviating that pain. But why would staff alleviate a pain they don't even know exists? Hence my belief that the individual assumes you see the pain yet you refuse to do anything about it. Think about it, the patient does not have to communicate they are hungry for the care provider to offer them food on a regular basis. They don't ask the care provider to get them up in the morning, get them dressed and off on the bus to day program. They don't ask to eat dinner or take a shower and then go to bed. All of these things are done automatically. Thus, the patient simply stands by being prompted to do this and that, and all of their needs are met for them. Why should pain be any different than any other need? If I have pain and need something done, it should happen on its own. When it doesn't and the pain becomes unbearable, who better to communicate my pain to than the care provider that I depend on the most? Hence the conclusion that they think we can see their pain. Behaviorally, this conclusion makes sense to me although I cannot provide any evidence of that. Few would agree that this is the case, though, especially since there is no evidence to support it. But I would argue that the evidence is there in the behavior; it just cannot be directly observed.

Further evidence supporting my conclusion is the fact that the developmentally disabled population, particularly the severely autistic or low functioning, noncommunicative individuals, do not learn to express pain the way you and I may express it. For example, if we had a toothache, we may actually put our hands up to our jaw on the same side that pain resides, make a facial grimace, and report that it hurts. If you don't learn these specific responses and are not even inclined to communicate to get any of your needs met, you won't have any facial expression or any other indications that you are in pain. So with no avenue to communicate and a behavioral pattern of simply waiting for needs to be met—and they usually are—before they become too uncomfortable, it is not difficult to conclude that they are waiting for you to act on it because they assume you know about it. But how would you know about it if you couldn't see it?

Reading Emotions

Researching this topic of reading emotions, I ran across Darwin's book *The Expression of the Emotions in Man and Animals*. An excerpt of the text goes as follows:

> The most striking case, though a rare and abnormal one, which can be adduced of the direct influence of the nervous system, when strongly affected, on the body, is the loss of colour in the hair, which has occasionally been observed after extreme terror or grief. One authentic instance has been recorded, in the case of a man brought out for execution in India, in which the change of colour was so rapid that it was perceptible to the eye.[1]

> Another good case is that of the trembling of the muscles, which is common to man and to many, or most, of the lower animals. Trembling is of no service, often of much disservice, and cannot have been at first acquired through the will, and then rendered habitual in association with any emotion. (Darwin, 1899)

This quote makes a couple of interesting points that indicate that not only do we express emotions physically, but also, we do so even when the behavior appears to have no survival value. Whether that is true or not, the point is that all animals have ways of expressing fear, anger, love, and acceptance, which are mediated

97

through the central nervous system and which, depending on the intensity of the emotion, become visible to other observers. Many of these emotions are beyond the control of the will, as he puts it. The implication is that many of us attempt to hide or mask our emotions by imposing our will on their expression, such as containing our excitement while buying a car in front of the salesman in the hopes of getting a better deal.

In the examples above, I have attempted to illustrate how emotions can be utilized in a functional analysis of behaviors and how these can possibly be used in the development of a behavior plan. But in the case of pain or other aversive and emotional experiences that could result in severe behavioral responses, it would be useful to know that these emotional states are building up in the individual so that something can be done about them before they result in physical aggression and extreme pain for the individual. Again, this is not science, but it is useful information in dealing with behavioral issues, especially for low-functioning and severely affected individuals who don't speak or speak but don't communicate. It is a biological fact that needs do not go away without some sort of action on the part of the individual, and it is something I often state and repeat to staff, that needs never go away, they simply get more intense. Thus, it is very useful to detect them building up as early as possible so that intervention can be implemented that will alleviate the need and avoid or prevent a serious behavioral episode. The following guidelines may help in diagnosing such a problem, or at least in detecting that there is a problem that requires further attention. These are all indicators, or red flags, that, if systematically followed up on, can lead to a problem that could possibly be defused before it becomes very intense and its expression dangerous to others around them.

Changes in Behavioral Pattern

The most common sign that something is wrong is a change in the usual behavioral pattern. That means that if you are new to the client, you would not be able to detect this antecedent to more serious behaviors. But as I mentioned above, behaviors are consistent and addictive. So in general, most people, developmentally disabled or not, do the same thing every day. For example, when one of my clients, whom I have a good rapport with, came home from the day program, he would usually put his lunch box down, smile at me, and want to talk. However, one day, when he came home and I was there, he dropped his lunch box off abruptly in the kitchen and went directly to his room. This was a surprise to me since he *always* wanted my attention. So I mentioned to staff that something must be wrong and I thought I would be going after him to see what the matter was. The staff warned me that he might attack me because this was the pattern as they saw it. I asked them to tell me about this pattern, and they responded by saying that when he came home upset, he would go to his room. By dinnertime, when they attempted to get him to come out, he would charge at the person and attempt to choke them. So I asked how long this interval between when he comes home and when dinnertime was, and the response was about an hour and forty-five minutes. It became clear to me what was happening. I quickly went to his room and expressed concern about him being upset. I directly addressed his problem rather than reprimanding him or teasing him about not greeting me because this would have escalated the situation. So I simply said, "Michael, what's wrong? You look like you're upset. Is there anything I can do to help you?" He bowed his head and would not respond. So I asked if he had a bad at the day program, and he nodded in the affirmative. I should mention that he is totally nonverbal but can write and use sign language. So I asked if he had gotten in trouble. He nodded in the negative. Then I asked again about what happened and why he was feeling so bad. He did not respond. So I asked him, "If I get you a piece of paper, will you write it down?" He simply looked at me. I took it to mean that he was not completely opposed to the idea. Once I got him the paper and pen, he wrote "Sup left." It turned out that it was his supervisor's last day at the job, and this was someone he was really attached to. So I consoled him and told him we may be able to track down her number where she was going and attempt to call her once in a while, or that probably she would come back on special occasions. I then talked to him about how sometimes people have to leave to get better jobs or have to move out of state, and that lots of things can happen that we cannot control. In short, after a while, he was fine and came out to the living room and resumed his normal routine, which consisted of cleaning out his lunch box to prepare it for the next day.

After this interaction, I spent some time with staff explaining to them that if they can see and read his behavior to the point of knowing he was upset, leaving him upset for an hour and forty-five minutes would only make things worse. Then I went through my mantra that "needs never go away, they simply get more intense" routine and instructed them to deal with the problem as soon as they detected it. This last point is a basic applied behavior analysis principle—to intervene as early as possible in the antecedent stage of the behavior. Although the staff had read his behavioral plan, they were simply following their gut feeling to leave him alone. But as I mentioned above, gut feelings alone are not adequate, just as behaviorism without accounting for feelings is sometimes not adequate. Both are necessary when dealing with emotional human beings. The key to utilizing this feature of behaviors is to be a good observer. Your eyes are the secret weapons. If you observe someone closely, you will see them very well and anticipate a problem because they are not acting like themselves.

Resistiveness-Isolation

Another thing to watch for that may indicate that something might be wrong is a general unwillingness to engage in activities that the individual usually would like to engage in. You may also see a lack of communication compared to their previous pattern. Oftentimes, they will self-isolate. A higher-functioning client may simply report they don't feel good. If this happens, you need to follow up on where it hurts. Usually, if the client is high functioning enough to tell you that they don't feel good, then they can indicate where it hurts, and your problem may be solved right there. However, in the case of emotional pain, such as the holidays coming up and knowing that all of the other clients will be going home except for them, then they won't be able to point to where the pain is, or, worse yet, they will point to their stomach or their head, thus making you conclude that it actually is some kind of stomachache when it isn't, or a headache that leads you to possibly give them some Tylenol or aspirin. One needs to be careful not to accept whatever the individual is reporting. We rarely have enough insight into our own behavior to know why we feel or do what we do, and developmentally disabled individuals are no different. We need to look at the wider context of the behavior. If an individual is acting differently, it is usually because something in their life, meaning environment, is different. In one of the cases above, we could see that the change was the change in supervisor at the workshop. In many cases, the environment will provide us with the answer as to why the individual is acting differently. And if we can see or guess at how they are feeling in relation to that change, we may have a better handle on what approach to use in dealing with the problem.

In the nonverbal client, one can attempt to diagnose the problem by going through the same procedure, but with the additional prompts of touching the individual. For example, although the individual may be nonverbal, they still do attend to verbal prompts. So you start by asking if anything hurts. Then you start by lightly touching the jaw area to rule out a toothache. If they don't respond, you can hold both sides of the jaw yourself to see if they attempt to get away or scream. If there is no apparent problem there, move to the stomach area and ask them if it hurts there. An impaction or bowel obstruction will usually result in a distended stomach that is hard to the touch. If that is the case, you must contact the nurse or take them to the doctor to possibly give them an enema to relieve the pain. If the stomach is not the problem, take their shoes and socks off and see if there are any ingrown toenails. And finally, when helping them with their shower or bath, do a body check to see if there are any bruises.

The point is to rule out all possible physiological problems with the individual before assuming that they are acting out. How you handle the behavior will be very different if you know that it is due to injury as opposed to it being due to resistiveness. What I am suggesting is that resistiveness is dependent on mood, and mood can be produced by physiological changes, even when we cannot pinpoint the problem.

Facial Reading

And last but not least is the practice of reading facial expressions. This requires some previous experience with the individual in question where you have seen them happy, seen them sad, etc., and know what kind of expression goes with what kind of emotion. But even without any experience, it is often possible to see sadness, anger, or happiness in facial expressions. Those expressions can be particularly helpful with the nonverbal population to tell when you should *not* attempt to engage them in activities. When a person is upset about something, the last thing they want is for someone to make additional demands on them. If someone appears upset about something, it is best to try to deal with it prior to attempting to get them involved with their daily chores or bathroom routine, or what have you. Sometimes it is possible to solve the problem without solving the problem simply by expressing concern about their situation and the fact that they don't feel good. Then you can introduce your agenda of getting them to engage in their routine as a helpful way to avoid feeling bad. Thus, you can tell them, "I know you feel bad about Alice leaving. I do too. But you know, you would probably feel better if you take a shower. You want me to help you?" In this way, you may be able to get them going with such a distraction. One that is familiar and soothing that may help them completely forget about whatever was bothering them.

Self-Monitoring

No discussion about emotions can be complete without discussing the issue of how your own behavior toward others provokes emotions. As mentioned earlier, emotions are the result of biochemical changes in the body that are aroused in the course of interacting with the environment. And one of the most powerful elements in the environment is others in the organism's species. All animals have an emotional reaction to seeing other members of their specie. The situation I am most exposed to is that of an environment where you have developmentally disabled individuals, and staff. Two distinctly different populations of people, and there is no mistake about who is who. Staff know they are there to run the place, and clients know who the staff are that get things done. What you observe in one of these settings is that there is a dance between these two populations: one that is frequently attempting to get the attention of the other and the other attempting to occupy and keep them busy so that they can implement their required agenda, whether it's running a class lesson, getting everyone ready for dinner, or getting everyone on the bus. It is very clear in these situations who is in charge. The clients being served are not the ones in charge. They are the recipients of care and instruction. Due to their disabilities, they have no means of getting things done without the help of the staff. Thus, getting the attention of staff is extremely important and vital for their mission. The staff have a completely different mission—to do as much as they can for all of the clients at once by engaging them in group activities, which is sometimes impossible given the variability of needs. Thus, it can be a hectic and trying event to make it through the day for both of them, the staff as well as the clients.

Within the context of the picture described above, getting the staff's attention for your own individual need is a prized commodity. Thus, there is a lot of emotional investment in getting the staff to attend to you. And when they don't, it creates an emotional disturbance in the client that can later be observed in the form of inappropriate behavior. When I give trainings to staff, I ask them to think about the following scenario: You are in your house, someone walks in, passes you as if you were not there, starts talking to another person for twenty minutes about their weekend—where they went, what they did, etc.—until it was time for dinner. Then all of a sudden, someone comes up to you and starts making demands such as, "Come on, let's wash our hands and get ready for dinner." The person, at that moment, resists and refuses to wash their hands. Why do you think that happens? Having done a great deal of functional analysis of behaviors such as these, it became apparent that when staff do not treat the clients with some respect and consideration, they will often not respond to their demands. While staff perceive themselves as not making any demands but simply requesting their cooperation, the developmentally disabled person is not appreciating the fact that this staff person did not even acknowledge them until they wanted to impose an agenda on them. You can observe that the staff who do take the time to greet them when they come in, talk to them, etc., have no problem once they start making requests of them. The way I view it is that behavior such as I just described amounts to symptoms of emotional neglect. I can actually see the hurt feelings in clients who follow an excited anticipation of seeing the staff walk in and continue walking. The look of excitement gives way to a frown of sadness.

I once was called to figure out what was wrong with Johnny. He was refusing to take a shower, and this has gone on three days in a row. After investigating the problem, I found out that Johnny has always taken his shower at 6:00 PM. However, ever since his house manager left on vacation, the substitute staff was attempting to shower him at 8:00 PM. But after waiting two hours for his usual shower, he was not happy and would refuse to go with staff to take his shower. Once we established what the problem was and staff began to shower him at 6:00 PM, the problem was solved. The most interesting thing, however, was Johnny's perception of the situation. I should mention that Johnny is an autistic individual that is very ritualistic. About a month after the situation just described, Johnny had one of his review meetings. He was sitting right next to me when I was giving my report on his behavior and was describing to the treatment team what went on about not showering him at 6:00 PM as usual; and as soon as I mentioned that, Johnny, while rocking as he usually does, said, "Yup, I guess they just don't love me." Now regardless of how we define love, the message is clear that when staff violate what the resident's routine is and what their expectation is, it is perceived as being somewhat uncaring, as if they did it on purpose to let him know they don't like him. No amount of explanation could resolve this problem. Only a change in behavior on the staff part could resolve this problem—simply by following the schedule as prescribed. This is particularly important in dealing with the autistic population, which seems to have great difficulty adapting to changes in daily routines.

In summary, emotions are quite important in the equation of the human experience and extremely relevant to behavior in general. People interpret our intentions all the time and react to them emotionally. In the example above, not following the set routine was not the only problem. Closer scrutiny would lead you to conclude that it is not that this person is autistic and simply unable to deal with changes, although that is partially true. But the change was implemented without his consent and approval. Not so much as an explanation was given as to why he could no longer get his shower at the regular time. Imagine if your boss at work simply changed your hours without your consent or notification but expected you to simply go with the program. Although that may happen, it would not be well received. When things are done to us that we do not expect, even if it is a good thing, it will require emotional resources to deal with that event. There are few people in the world, if at all, that would not experience an emotional reaction to such a change. Thus, when dealing with others, it is extremely important to monitor the effect you are having on them and adjust your presentation and interaction on their reactions to your behavior. Usually, this is a reciprocal process. However, when you are dealing with developmentally disabled people, especially if they are blind, that reciprocity is not quite as fluid and is usually a one-way street. It is us who must monitor and adjust our behavior because some disabled people do not have the resources to reciprocate or the ability to monitor and interpret our behaviors.

This process of reciprocity is essential for live performers. For a performer to adequately work the room, they must go with whatever the mood of the room is, usually through careful observation of the behavior of the audience. The better the performer can do this, the more they respond to and engage in the performance. This is another instance of reading emotions. It is a necessary and important social skill. We diagnose individuals lacking these nonverbal social skills as having Asperger's syndrome. I would argue that nonverbal social skills are the same as what I am suggesting as being able to read emotions or work the room in that in both cases, we are watching for and interpreting the behaviors of others in reaction to us and our own behavior and make changes to our own behaviors based on those reactions or our interpretation of them.

Manipulation Not Accommodation

Let me clarify that the purpose of utilizing emotional parameters in a functional analysis is *not* meant to mean that we should accommodate or pander to people's emotions when they occur. Rather, we need to become familiar with them to eliminate their expression in the current form. Thus, when a person has tantrums because they feel embarrassed, I am not suggesting that the interventionist should attend to the behavior by apologizing to the person for embarrassing them. The consequence, as I will describe later in the intervention chapter, cannot be a response that facilitates the emotion, but one that will hopefully discourage the behavior from being repeated. Thus, the purpose of familiarizing ourselves with the emotional state behind the behavior is so that we have a hint as to what a behavioral plan should accomplish for the individual that will be the recipient of it. In other words, we have an idea as to what we want the individual to feel as a result of the intervention. Do we want the individual to feel more in control, more empowered by communicating their needs more appropriately, to feel that they are being treated fairly or that their opinion matters? Guessing as to what the subject may be feeling will give us a hint as to how we should proceed in the development of a behavioral plan.

CHAPTER 8

What Guides Behavior

Ergonomics and Reciprocity

Although all of us have many ways in which we can meet any one of our particular needs, there are several parameters that are quite relevant in reference to which one of those behaviors we will engage in. We've already discussed that behaviors are determined by needs and fueled by discomfort or *emotion*. But we have yet to discuss what forces are at play in determining the shape and type of behavior that will be exhibited. Some of those forces will undoubtedly include the immediate environment, what options that environment presents in relation to the need that is being expressed at that moment, and prior learning in how to meet that need. But the most inherent force that guides behavior from a behavioral sociobiological perspective is the force of *ergonomics* as it shapes behavior through reciprocity—the motivation to behave in the most expedient way possible (motivation). Motivation and emotion are required topics of courses in psychology, no matter what kind of psychology one is studying. A major preoccupation of psychology is to answer the questions, "Why did she do that?" and "What made him do that?" While we have discussed emotions in the previous chapters, I now turn to the topic of motivation. While emotions are the raw material that provokes or fuels behavior, motivation is the guiding force that determines the face of behavior—that part that we can all see or at least infer from behavior.

Ergonomics is similar to economics in the sense that both attempt to solve a problem by a solution that minimizes the amount of effort necessary to achieve the desired result and maximizes profits, which would be the amount of the desired result. *Ergonomics* is a word derived from the Greek words *ergon*, which means "work" or "effort," and *nomos*, which means "law" or "surroundings." The field of work safety is full of ergonomic ideas and theories of work safety. However, the concept is here used as an underlying force of biological entities that is concerned with meeting needs with the least amount of effort or energy expenditure based on what is available in the immediate environment.

One can design a simple experiment to illustrate this concept in the following way (see fig. 7 below): Take any animal and present them with a forced-decision maze setup as depicted below—whereby you present them with two paths, one long and one short, both leading to the same prize, something that the organism wants, and you run ten or twenty trials. At some point, whether by curiosity or some other need, the organism will explore both routes but will eventually settle on one—usually, the shortest route or the one that requires the least amount of energy to expend to get the prize or reinforcer.

This simple experiment illustrates the principle of ergonomics as it pertains to behavior. In a more formal treatment of this subject, one can characterize the process by the following equation:

$$C-/B+$$

where C = cost and B = benefit.

What I am referring to is the energy expenditure of the organism in question. As I mentioned earlier, when we experience a need, we would like to meet that need in the fastest and easiest way possible. Thus, one of the primary driving forces of behavior is this principle of ergonomics. Organisms do not want to expend energy needlessly. So the organism is always on the lookout for a shortcut, an easier way to do whatever they have to do repeatedly.

This process occurs automatically and without any real effort on the part of the organism, at least not intentional effort that is goal oriented. For example, when first learning to drive a car, the person in the driver's seat is expending a great deal of energy to try to stay on the road, look at the rearview mirrors and use the brakes probably more than they should, and drive at a low speed. In fact, after a short drive, the person is tired and drained of energy and is relieved they are no longer behind the wheel. That same person, if they simply continue to drive without any further instructions, will begin to drive better and spend less energy doing so. This is true of playing the piano, engaging in sports, cooking, or whatever behavior that requires a great deal of behavioral movements with the intent of accomplishing a specific result. What is happening here is that as the individual performs these series of movements, their behavior is reinforced by the results of their behavior, which is then shaped and refined to abandon those physical movements that are irrelevant or interfere with the desired result, and keep as well as perfect those physical movements that maximize the effectiveness of reaching that desired result. It is as if the organism automatically and without intentional learning is shaping their own behavior through interaction with the environment. This is another example of *reciprocity* mentioned above, which is another driving force in the production of behavior.

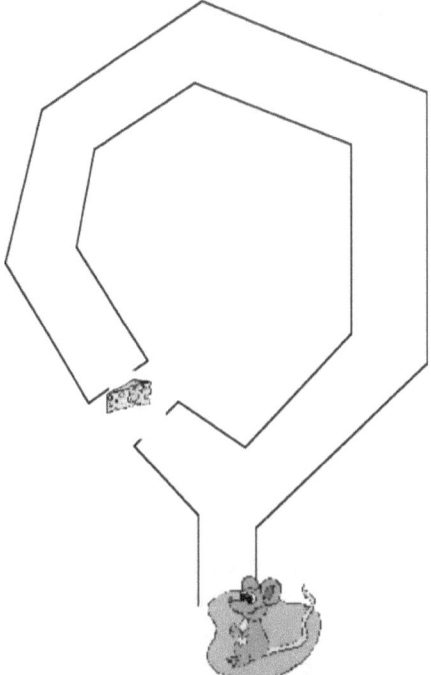

Figure 7: Hypothetical forced decision maze experiment

The implication of this phenomenon on learning is that learning does *not* require that the organism, through its mental capacities, figure out what needs to be done and do it, as is usually depicted in the field of human learning and education. Anyone can learn about playing the guitar, but to play the guitar is something completely different. Learning any skill requires this interactional reciprocity but does not necessarily require a lot of cognitive restructuring or even information about the act to be performed. That is why practice makes perfect, because if you keep doing the same task over and over, your body learns how to implement those movements faster, smoother, and with less energy. Thus, through reciprocity and ergonomics, behaviors are shaped and become more efficient, and this occurs with or without cognitive intervention or interpretation.

The motivational implications of this process are obvious from an evolutionary standpoint. Accomplishing tasks with the least amount of energy expenditure is beneficial to the organism and can improve its chances for survival. There is less wear and tear on the system, and their needs get met when needed with no unnecessary delays. No one is exempt from or escapes the forces of ergonomics and reciprocity. No matter who you are and what you are doing, if you are doing it repeatedly, you will get better at it, faster at doing it, and do it with less energy output. It is a hidden motivational force that can very effectively be used in behavioral intervention, as we shall see later. And again, this aspect of behavior is not learned. Ergonomics appears to be an essential feature of biological organisms in general.

Social Viability

In any specie that we can talk about, the group structure evolves around those that are dominant and those that are passive in such a way as to consist of a few leaders and many followers. The leaders will then set the rules or, more specifically, decide on what is and what is not acceptable behavior within the group structure. And the followers will have to behave accordingly or face the consequences. A complete accounting of how this occurs is far beyond the scope of this book, and we are only concerned here with the existence of that structure and how it affects individual behavior within the group. The point I would like to emphasize is that due to the development of this structure, which has many substructures and subgroups, where the few control the many, behavioral options for meeting needs is narrowed arbitrarily, based on the needs of the leaders, which may have little to do with the needs of the followers and indeed occurs at the expense of the followers.

For example, although we may be able to attract a member of the opposite sex in many different ways, cultural and group constraints severely limit many of these possibilities. I am here focusing on sexual behavior because it is probably one of the most ritualized of any class of behaviors, and this is particularly true of humans. In nonhuman species, these rituals can be quite elaborate but are much more uniform within the specie than in the variety of human cultures. And controlling or exerting pressure to behave in certain ways concerning such a vital and important function of biological entities can significantly control and limit the prosperity, survivability, and reproductive ability of individuals within the group structure. As mentioned earlier, overcoming the social group structure that one is born into is possible but can be difficult, if not impossible, for some. Thus, the need for group action of the many against the few so that the barriers to participation in the social structure are equalized and assured access is guaranteed to all. Although this is a democratic principle, it is rarely adhered to due to the corrupting influence of money and power, which restrict access to those who have the money and those who are connected to the power structure. What I am suggesting is that political action is the main avenue to widening and equalizing the viability of social options for all. And this action requires group effort.

Generally, those born within a certain class remain within that class or rise a little above where they were, regardless of talent and potential for growth. Again, there are ways to overcome this limitation, but the effort required is sometimes prohibitive and the individual is not that motivated, especially if they are content with their current situation. Discomfort or discontent in one's own group structure is the key to overcoming that structure. The discomfort will provide the fuel and motivation to rise above the current circumstances, simply to find more circumstances to deal with. Thus, the ergonomics of the situation in combination with the level of discontent will determine how far one will go in climbing the social ladder. As mentioned above, reciprocity is extremely important in this discussion. Because the existing social structure will exert pressure on the individual to comply despite their own needs and self-interests, overcoming these barriers will depend on the ergonomic opportunities and reciprocal effect provided by the environment in relation to the intensity of the individual's internal state. Some of us are much more motivated to fight that fight, either due to having more energy, drive, and discomfort, or the opportunity to do so.

Education

In reference to behavior, formal education seems to have little in the way of causing behavioral change. I am not suggesting that education does not alter some behavioral responses such as the vocation one engages in or the economic status that will affect behavior, but in reference to transformational change. For example, if one liked music before they had an education, that won't significantly change as a result of education. However, if one loved music, entered the music industry, and had very bad and negative experiences in that industry, he or she may actually change in feeling as well as behavior in relation to the music they once loved. What I am suggesting is that change resulting from education is minimal compared to actual experiential learning through reinforcement or nonreinforcement of efforts. Education simply provides us with information and the paperwork necessary to enter certain fields, and these vocations may, in time, transform our thinking and behavior through the experiences we become subjected to. Education in the formal sense has little to do with behavioral change. Education in the experiential form is what alters behaviors.

You can see the limited effect education has on behavior by simply asking yourself, how much have you retained from your formal education and how often does that affect your daily routine? For example, most of us had to learn all of the capitals of the United States in grade school. How many of you still know them? I would guess few of us still know them. Formal education, while

I strongly believe in, only affects behavior when actually applied in the world outside the academic institutions in which it was obtained.

Education can also be viewed as simply an extension of the social structure. Thus, instead of being facilitative to change, many actually discourage change and innovation. In many ways, education can actually stifle transformational change in behavior. I have had many professors who penalized novelty and radical thinking. I know within my own experience that formal education had little to do with any behavioral change. Those experiences that resulted in behavioral change were meaningful experiences of interaction with others—and usually others that were not from my own group or class. I will now focus on this last and most important agent of behavioral change—interactional experiences.

Experience

They say, "Necessity is the mother of all invention." The implication is that need provokes behavioral change. In the strict interpretation of applied behavior analysis, the only behaviors that are ever learned are those behaviors that have been reinforced and thus have a functional relationship to our survival and our existence. For a behavior to be reinforced, it must first occur. Thus, all learning is experiential in nature. We don't learn by reading books and listening to instructions from others. That is simply accumulation of information, much of which will soon be lost. We learn by doing, experiencing the result of our behavior; and if the result is a positive one, we repeat that behavior in the future. But if the result or consequence of our behavior is negative, we will avoid engaging in that behavior in the future. This simplistic explanation of behavior does hold true but is not the whole story. Because even this simplistic view of behavior implies that all learning is experiential.

Experiences are quite varied in their impact on the individual, at least in reference to how the experience will affect their behavior. There are those experiences that are transformative to the individual and will affect many aspects of the organism's behavioral pattern and those experiences that will result in minute changes in behavior that occur only in very restricted contexts.

For example, the experience of learning to tie your shoes will change your behavior in reference to tying your shoes, maybe once a day for a couple of minutes. Thus, the behavioral impact on how that individual behaves throughout the day is quite small and restricted. On the other hand, finding out that one has cancer with little chance of recovery will probably have a much higher impact on the behavioral routine of the individual experiencing it. The change will involve the entire person and their daily routine. The person will focus on completely different things in light of this new information even though the only thing that led to this tremendous change is some information from another person, a doctor. In actual fact, behaviorally, learning to tie your shoes is more experiential than simply hearing a few words from another human being. The difference is what we make of the stimuli we are subjected to. Although there were many more stimuli and a prescribed sequence of behaviors to learn how one ties their shoes, and very little experiential learning involved in hearing a diagnosis, the resulting future behavior change is enormous for one and very small for the other.

As I just illustrated, behavior change can be the result of low—or high-intensity stimulation from the environment on our hypothetical gradient. But this level of stimulation has almost no relationship with the intensity of effect the stimulation has on the person experiencing it. Take for example a porn star having sex. That act may have no significant effect on the individual and may not be very exciting at all. But the same act to an individual who has never experienced sexual intercourse could be quite transformative to the point of them being willing to change their whole life as a result of that experience. The important point here is that although the environment shapes our behavior, it does so only to the extent that it has an effect on us. Thus, it is not the environment alone that is doing the job. The result of the behavior change depends on what is already inherent in the individual. What is inherent in the individual is not directly observable but inferred from observation. Again, we return to the private world of the organism experiencing the environment. But I would argue that the environment simply provides opportunities to engage in behavior. It is the organism and their current internal state of need that is neurologically, chemically, and biologically impacted, which determines the level of impact the environment will have on them, if any. These parameters are becoming more and more observable with the increasing rate at which technologies are being developed.

In the field of applied behavior analysis, many believe that the environment holds the answers to all things behavioral. I would suggest that this is only partially true. For example, if I love pastrami sandwiches and I happen to be in the presence of the best pastrami sandwich in the world, whether I respond to it or not will largely depend on how full I am, when was the last time I ate, whether I am currently experiencing indigestion, and whether I have my antacids with me or not. So although the environment is providing me with an opportunity to engage in a very high-probability behavior that is quite reinforcing, it does not necessarily provoke the anticipated or expected response if my physiological state is not in a receptive mode to process this stimuli. What is outside the organism must match what is on the inside of the organism for the behavior chain to occur. The law of reciprocity still holds true. This does not mean that the environment does not matter. It matters very much, especially when the organism is in a certain state of deprivation, which can be produced by the environment, in time. Thus, being aware of these internal parameters can actually improve the controlling effect of applied behavior analysis. And if this is true, why would we not want to pay attention to these internal variables? For example, when setting up a reinforcement schedule for individuals, one must pay attention to prevent the satiation effect of that individual. The level of satiation is different for each individual and must be evaluated and adjusted as the data reveals once intervention begins. Again, it is *not* an environmental parameter solely. All environmental effects depend on the immediate and current state of the individual's own physiology and need state. We don't all need the same amount of attention, reinforcement, or instruction to learn something. The degree of need determines the degree of impact the environment will have on us.

CHAPTER 9

Precursors of Intervention

What Scenario Is This Anyway

Before embarking on an intervention plan, it is important to consider what type of situation you are dealing with. Rarely is it a singular specific behavior that is the problem, such as smoking, where all we have to do is devise ways to avoid, discourage, and develop alternatives to the behavior. That would be rather simple. In many cases, the problem is more complex only in that the parameters that have created the problem are not accessible to the interventionist. Those parameters are largely emotional in nature and have to do with separation issues, abandonment issues, anger issues, and previous years of reinforcement for inappropriate behavior, as well as strong dependencies on others to meet their needs. Once they get to me, they are usually in adulthood, because it is at that point that they become more dangerous and unmanageable. It is easy to deal with a five-year-old that has a tantrum and throws a few toys around. It is entirely a different situation when it is an adult overturning tables and throwing chairs at others when angry and they weigh 260 pounds, or more. But once the individual is taken away from the environment that produced and reinforced these behaviors, they become disoriented as to what is and what is not acceptable behavior since the new environment is not responding to their behaviors in the same manner that the previous environment did.

As we have seen in the revenge case in chapter 5, once the individual was able to sufficiently satisfy his emotional need for imposing justice on others who have wronged him, a behavioral plan was no longer necessary. If you will remember, the original plan was to have him exercise some self-control, and he could earn a lunch outing with me once a month, provided he did not assault anyone. However, once he could take care of the problem and assure himself that he caused and inflicted a consequence on someone who did something to him that he shouldn't have, the plan was no longer necessary. Thus, the formal plan is reduced from formal to informal, meaning that staff no longer have to chart the behavior but keep the plan in mind to remind the individual should he begin escalating. Once this goes on for six months to a year, the intervention plan is deleted as met. This case would be the best scenario where the plan is temporary, focused, and successful to the point of not being necessary.

In the case of the girl who was depressed after her mother passed away, there were plans in place that were effective in dealing with her various behaviors, but these plans no longer worked once her mother had passed away. And if you will remember, the turnaround event was a strong relationship with one particular staff member. Thus, the intervention plan worked, but required the additional emotional support for it to be effective. It is as if she needed to have someone to impress or be proud of her for her to achieve and earn her reinforcers. When no such person existed in her life, the reinforcers were not effective. Thus, the conclusion I reached was that it was not earning the reinforcer that was important but, rather, demonstrating to a significant other that she could earn it; and it was this aspect that was reinforcing. This scenario is a little more difficult in that these artificial goals that I need to set up for her to show that she can meet them are more long-term and keep her dependent on others. The reality is that some individuals are more dependent on others, and this is true whether they are developmentally disabled or not. The goal of all intervention is to discontinue treatment and have the inappropriate behavior remain absent. In many cases, I have not been successful at achieving this result. The second-best thing is to have a plan that works and keep it in place indefinitely.

Then there are those cases that, for one reason or another, are not responsive to any intervention plan or marginally responsive. Those are the cases of chronic and severe self-injurious behavior or severe and intense agitation that results in aggressive behaviors. It has been my experience that these cases fall into two categories:

- those that have had a very long history of reinforcement for inappropriate behavior
- those that are chemically imbalanced and mostly not responsive to environmental contingencies in general

The former tend to be the aggressive type, and the latter tend to be the self-injurious type. This is an oversimplification of the situation, but the important point here is that we often encounter individuals that do not respond to or attend to the environment and, as a consequence, do not improve apparently because they get more reinforcement from their self-injurious behavior, which is frequently self-stimulatory in nature, than we are able to provide for them in the form of a tangible reinforcer. These individuals are the ones that are chemically imbalanced. The agitated types that have been reinforced for tantrums and assaults by giving them what they want due to fear that they will assault you are extremely difficult to treat since not giving them what they want produces even more violent and dangerous explosive episodes. In both of these cases, intervention alone is usually not as effective since we cannot come up with a replacement behavior, for example, that will match the intensity of pulling off all of their toenails in one sitting, just as we cannot tolerate the agitated client who will destroy an entire house in a few minutes as well as hurt themselves and others in the process because they are not given what they want. These are cases where psychotropic medications are needed in addition to a structured behavioral plan that can teach them more appropriate replacement behaviors and keep them calm enough and safe enough to learn those replacement behaviors. And as they become more and more proficient at exhibiting these replacement behaviors, titration of the medications can begin.

Ergonomics II

Before discussing the topic of changing behavior more specifically, we must first return to the subject of ergonomics. You will remember from the previous chapter that ergonomics is a driving force for all organisms. Let me remind you of the little mouse in figure 7. Note that I concluded by stating the rat will find and settle on the short rather than the long route to get the piece of cheese. So what does this have to do with changing behavior? I'm glad you asked, because I am going to tell you. What we see in experiments such as these, as mentioned above, is that the organism will engage in the behavior that is obviously the easiest to execute. And as mentioned earlier in reference to the features of behaviors, they are communicative in intent, and they must serve a purpose. So we can view inappropriate behaviors, which are the focus of our intervention efforts, as inappropriate ways to communicate needs and inefficient ways to meet needs. I must point out that in the forced decision maze, the answer is quite obvious and simple to learn. In real life, it is rarely that obvious, especially if you have a disability that interferes with your cognitive functions. So if a child learns through experience that if they don't like what's going on, they have a tantrum and the result is that they are removed from the situation, the child will continue to do that. This is *not* a cognitive process necessarily but, rather, an experiential one. The child learns that when things get too tense, too loud, or too something, tantrums provide them with the escape from that situation. After many years of doing this, it is difficult to simply inform the child that they no longer have to do this and that all they have to do is indicate to you that they don't want to be there. What we want to achieve in any behavioral plan is for the subject to discover the short end of the maze, as the mouse has. To do so, we utilize what we know about ergonomics. You will remember the equation of cost/benefit noted here again:

$$C-/B+$$

According to ergonomics, the child or adult exhibiting the inappropriate behavior is engaging in behavior that *is* the lowest-cost response for the highest benefit they are seeking. For example, in the case of the child or adult having a tantrum when under stress—which is a common reaction of autistic or anxious individuals in loud, noisy, crowded, or closed spaces—the individual has learned an automatic reaction to have a tantrum as soon as they feel the stress to escape. It is a habit, and addiction, as mentioned earlier as the feature of repetitive responses. As we will shortly see, there are behavioral indicators and observable antecedents to this behavior. But for now, let me point out that ergonomically speaking, a tantrum may not be the most efficient way of communicating discomfort and the need to escape. But given their history and behavioral repertoire, this is the only behavior they know that always achieves escape. So to teach them a replacement behavior, we must do so by using ergonomics to teach them how to find the short route to the piece of cheese, so to speak. This is done by introducing two contingencies at the same time that will have the ergonomic relationship shown in figure 8 below. The top box depicts what the subject is doing at the present time. Thus, we should read the top box as "Exhibiting a tantrum is the lowest-cost response that the subject can make to achieve the benefit of escape." The intervention plan should now introduce two contingencies: one that will discourage the behavior and one that will reinforce a replacement behavior that is less costly than the original behavior but achieves the same end.

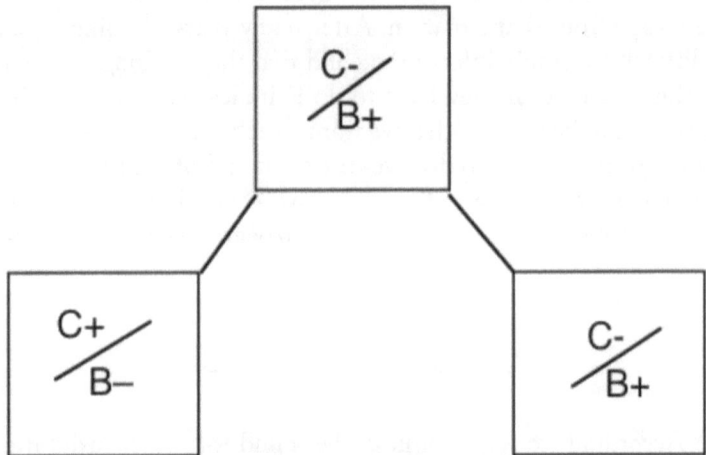

Figure 8: The two contingency plans

Let us take this one at a time. First, the behavior being exhibited of having a tantrum is extremely inefficient in communicating the subject's need. It requires effort and a great deal of energy to accomplish. It also upsets others, and probably the person exhibiting the behavior as well. We can compare this to the mouse taking the long way around the maze to get the cheese because they don't see the short way. So we want to teach a replacement behavior that is more efficient, and we will use ergonomics to help us because it taps into the natural tendency to want to achieve the most economical way of getting what we want with the least amount of effort. So the two contingency plans would, on the lower left box, increase the cost and reduce the benefit. This is achieved by preventing escape when the behavior is exhibited. When you prevent escape, you are reducing the benefit, which is to escape. When you do this, you are also increasing the cost because when you prevent escape, the subject will continue to exhibit the tantrum and expend more energy. This motivates the person to engage in a different behavior, which is what we want. The different behavior will be the replacement behavior and the second contingency of the plan.

Now we turn to the lower right box in figure 8, which is, ironically, the right response we want the subject to exhibit instead of the tantrum behavior. Since we have already assumed that the functional analysis has revealed that escape is the function, we want to teach the subject to escape more effectively. To do so will depend on the communicative abilities of the person in question. If they can talk, the replacement behavior is to teach them to say, "Break, please!" If they are nonverbal, they can make the sign for *break*, or simply point to the door. This behavior has a lower energy requirement, thus less cost, and achieves the same end or benefit, which is escape.

Now that we have described the various elements of the plan, let me illustrate how such a plan will actually be implemented in the real world. First of all, as I mentioned in chapter 4 on the features of behaviors, behaviors are addictive and habit forming. Thus, putting *any* plan in place will necessitate a change in habit, and this is not easy. Rarely do we get the results mentioned in the revenge case, where once they understood or changed their perception, the problem disappeared. In most cases, progress is slow and requires repeated exposures. To facilitate this process, I will actually walk the reader through the actual intervention as it *should* occur.

The first step is to inform the subject. Whether verbal or nonverbal, you should communicate as best as you can, using as few words as possible, what should happen. Thus, you let the individual know that you will be going to the mall. You might say, "I know you don't like the mall, but I cannot leave you by yourself. But if you feel that you need to leave, you have to tell me by either making the sign for break or saying, 'Break, please!' and I will take you outside for a while." Just telling the person this will probably not result in any behavioral change. Because again, as mentioned in chapter 4, behaviors tend to be automatic responses to stimuli that have been reinforced by such stimuli in the past. So the interventionist is simply setting the stage by communicating the intervention to the subject. Now once inside the mall, which is the antecedent for tantrum behavior, the interventionist must pay close attention to the other antecedents of the behavior. These would include behavioral signs of anxiety or agitation, such as rocking while walking, walking faster, engaging in hand flapping while walking, and different facial expressions. If the interventionist does not observe any of those signs, they may want to occasionally ask the person if they are doing OK and see what their response is. As soon as any signs of agitation occur, the interventionist should begin prompting the subject to exhibit the appropriate behavior. Thus, the interaction would begin by the interventionist asking, "Are you getting upset?" or "Is this too much for you? Do you need a break?" If they respond by making the sign or saying it, immediately remove them from the area so as to reinforce that behavior instead of the tantrum. However, if you miss the antecedents or they simply don't exhibit identifiable antecedents—which is rare—and tantrum, then the interventionist should begin prompting them to make the appropriate response to escape and attempt to not allow escape until the response is made. Too often, staff become embarrassed and simply take them out, much as a mom may buy her child that candy bar to avoid a scene at the checkout counter rather than teach appropriate behavior. This is the wrong response. If you do this, you will be reinforcing the tantrum behavior.

A couple of things to keep in mind: Intervene in the antecedent cycle as soon as possible. If you wait too long, you will risk the behavior occurring and reinforcing a habit that is already there and make behavior change even harder since you are developing a history of the subject doing this in your presence. The other point is that learning occurs faster when the reinforcement comes immediately after the response. Any delays will interfere with and delay learning. Thus, you *must* immediately take them out as soon as they indicate the need to leave.

Attacking the Center

In my own research on compliance training, I found that compliance for some of my subjects was what Rincover coined as a *keystone behavior* (Cayem, 1986). A keystone behavior is one that, when modified, could facilitate change in numerous behaviors for which no systematic contingency has been applied (Rincover, 1981). Russo had coined the term *response covariance* to explain this phenomenon (Russo et al., 1981). Thus, as one behavior varied in response to intervention, other behaviors varied without any specific interventions. It has been my experience that such is the case for many individuals I have worked with. Those who have an issue with compliance are those who generally don't like being told what to do. Being told what to do provokes an emotional reaction that results in noncompliance. This noncompliance can escalate to self-injurious behavior, aggression, and property destruction. For others, it is approval that is essential, as was the case with the girl who functioned best when she had a significant other to impress and bond with.

A behaviorist does not always formally address every behavior that the referral source complains about. In choosing which behaviors to address, the most severe and disruptive behaviors are usually the ones that are targeted. However, those may not be the keystone behaviors. The interventionist should keep in mind what is important for that particular client. Some of this information can come from the reinforcement survey (see Reinforcement Survey in the appendix). Additional information can be derived from interviews with people that know the subject well. The important thing to find out is, what is the agenda of that particular person? Do they want to be cool? Do they want approval? Do they want to be treated as important to the group? Do they like to lead? Those are all emotional needs that are often marginalized or completely ignored in the development of a behavior plan. I would argue that these are the most important in developing a unified general approach to intervention. As mentioned earlier, although human emotions can be numerous and complex, they do fall into general categories, and there are a great deal of similarities between subjects in reference to those general emotional categories. Thus, we get the bully, the shy one, the one that's always helpful, etc., and attempt to meet those general styles of behavior by speaking to them in their own language. The three examples below will illustrate what I mean. However, let me mention that I am not attempting to provide you with a specific plan for any behavior, but simply pointing to approaches that can be utilized in a general sense for those types of individuals. In the real world, you would have to customize these approaches to fit the particular person you are working with. For example, when I talk about reinforcement, this could be anything from earning the privilege of vacuuming the carpet to going to Disneyland. I will discuss later on how to choose a reinforcer.

The Boss

One common type of individual exhibiting behavioral problems in a social setting—such as a classroom, a dorm, or a day program—is the boss. For the person that bosses others and is somewhat a bully, the intervention plan should find ways to make that individual in charge of things, which would consist of whatever that individual can handle within that setting. And this "job" would be considered very seriously and would be contingent upon appropriate execution of the duties of that job. Reinforcement in the form of verbal praise and recognition can be provided, in addition to the already-obvious benefits of having the individual feel like they are in charge and important to the group. These elements of a behavior plan should be included for *all* behavioral problems exhibited by this individual. As discussed above, the keystone behavior in this case would be taking charge of the situation. So the obvious replacement behavior is to provide them with the charge they are seeking so long as they practice appropriate skills in executing their role. Thus, instead of reprimanding the individual or threatening their reinforcement earnings when they engage in their inappropriate bossing behavior, you engage in a job performance evaluation. Then you have them practice the appropriate behavior to show you that they understand.

Let me not underestimate the importance of tangible earnings for doing the job. Again, we will be discussing what should be considered when choosing reinforcers. But generally speaking, "What's in it for me?" is a question that we *all* ask ourselves all the time. Thus, if you are expecting an individual to behave differently, you better give them a good reason to do so.

The Princess

This is the girl who has been somewhat spoiled by her parents. She gets whatever she wants by smiling, pleading, and pouting. A girl like that will need a lot of affection and approval from her social group. However, she will have to obtain it by engaging in different behaviors. Specifically, she needs to be more with her peer group rather than with her parents since her peer group is much less likely to respond to her emotional ploys than her parents who truly love her. For such an individual, it would be cruel to completely stop all signs of affection and make her quit cold turkey in the new environment. It would be better to attack this situation by slowly limiting access to parents with their consent and approval and immersing her in positive social environments such as going to dances where she can dress up, the glee club, a theater arts group, and possibly a painting class. Anything that will produce social reinforcement and acceptance will do. A person like that is used to approval, and thus, we must teach her how to get approval in a world without her parents. This process can often take several years, but the transition can eventually be made with the cooperation of the parents.

The Cool Guy

This is a person who sees themselves as hip, with it, and cool. Thus, in dealing with such individuals, it is important to find out what kind of music they like and what kind of clothes go with that style of music. Motivating such individuals is easy with concerts, CDs, music videos, etc., that make them feel like they are part of that movement. Individuals like that are also highly motivated by trinkets that reflect their taste, such as wearing bling-bling around their neck or getting particular T-shirts with their favorite band on it. Reprimanding inappropriate behavior should always be framed in the language of "not being cool to do that" or "cool guys would not do that" as motivators to stop engaging in inappropriate behavior.

I could go on and on about types of individuals I have worked with, but the intention here is not to provide you with an inventory of types but, rather, point out the global aspect of a behavior plan, which precedes the specific plan that will eventually be developed. This global approach to dealing with behaviors, I found, is extremely effective in getting staff to remember the behavioral plans of all the people they serve. It is often the global and general approach that is remembered rather than the specifics of a behavioral plan that staff remembers. Thus, when I am training staff about intervention, I spend little time on the specific plans and spend much more time on describing the general person and what turns them on so that even if a new behavior crops up that does not yet have a plan, they have a general idea as to what approach to take. If we cannot find some way to spark the individual's interest in buying into our plan, we will make little progress in shaping behavior. Often, the most important element in a behavior plan is the person implementing that plan. If that person is sensitive to the needs of the individual who is the recipient of that plan, progress is swift. If that person sees themselves as the instructor and looks down on the client as someone that needs to be put in their place when they exhibit an inappropriate behavior, then not only is there no progress, but one can see an escalation in behaviors. Thus, we cannot underestimate the power of the *relationship*.

The Relationship

In studying the relationship between staff and client to determine what are the operative elements that facilitate learning, I found several patterns of interaction that promote a good relationship. In implementing any behavior plan, *attitude* is of the utmost importance. First of all, the interventionist should not take responsibility for anything having to do with the plan. By this I mean that the person actually implementing the intervention should never personalize the consequences as if they are the product of the interventionist. For example, if an individual is on a program to earn a soda for cleaning up their room and fail to do so but claim that they have and want the soda anyway, the interventionist is *not* to respond by stating, "You did not clean your room, so I am not giving you the soda." This response implies that the individual's job is to satisfy you rather than simply do their job. It would be much more effective and productive to say something like, "Well, I see that you missed a few things, so why don't you go ahead and finish the job so that you can earn the soda." The idea is that the interventionist should *stay neutral.* They are not to punish or reward based on whether they are pleased or displeased with the results. They are to help the individual earn their pay by doing their job. So whether the person earns their soda or not is not their responsibility. Staff should not be nagging them to do it. If an individual decides that it is good enough and they should get the soda, the interventionist should simply state the rules such as pointing out that cleaning the room requires that all clothes are off the floor and put away but that there are still clothes on the floor. If they refuse to pick up the clothes, you simply inform them of what the rules are, namely, that when clothes are left on the floor, the job has not been done and the soda cannot be earned because that is what their job is, *not* because the interventionist did not like the way the person cleaned the room. The interventionist must impress upon the individual that they are simply following the rules of the plan because that is their job. If the person wants to earn the soda, the interventionist is there to help them do so by letting them know what they have to do to earn it.

Personalizing whether the individual has earned their reinforcer or not must be based on clear outcomes that can easily be pointed out. What the interventionist thinks about what is or is not a good job *is not* the intent of the plan. The interventionist should not claim any reward or blame for whether the client did or did not earn the soda. That is the job of the plan itself. If the plan is not working, it should be changed. But the responsibility of the interventionist is to simply follow the plan. In this way, it avoids the client believing that it is the interventionist that is mean, and that is why they are not getting their soda, especially if other interventionists who work with them allow them to do a sloppy job. Thus the importance of clarity in the definitions used to describe outcomes just as it is in describing behaviors. When delivering a negative consequence, such as informing a client that they cannot go on the outing because they did not do such and such that they were supposed to do, the interventionist can express a sorry rather than a punitive tone to avoid being the recipient of the client's rage or discontent. Thus, staff may say, "Johnny, I am really sorry you won't be able to come with us to the park, but maybe you can earn the next outing if you can remember not to hit Sally." Disapproval does not need to be added to the consequence. They are already paying for their mistake with the consequence. You don't want to add your disproval to it. Doing so will only let the client know what upsets you. So that when you do something they don't like in the future, they will repeat that behavior to get you back. The interventionist should never allow the client to see what upsets them for that reason. If you have an effective plan, you should not have to exhibit approval or disapproval. A generally *supportive* role is what is essential in the relationship. Thus, if the client did not earn something, the interventionist should work with the client to make sure they earn it the next time. In this way, the client is unable to blame the interventionist for earning or not earning their reinforcement. The interventionist should *stay positive*, even when delivering a negative consequence. This will communicate to the client that it is their responsibility whether they earn or not their reinforcer. The interventionist is simply *following the rules* of the plan.

I must mention arousal in reference to delivering reinforcement or consequences. In implementing these contingencies, the amount of arousal used is quite significant. Staff, or the interventionist, should minimize arousal in implementing consequences, and maximize arousal in delivering reinforcers. Thus, the response for delivering consequences should be muted and factual as to why they did not earn whatever it was they were working for. However, when the client does a good job, the response should be animated, a little loud, and a little repetitive. So you may tell them they did a good job in several ways such as "That was great! I think that is the best you've done so far. I can't believe you did it all on your own too, with no one telling you what to do. That is a great job! I'm proud of you!" The reason why I emphasize the arousal aspect is that it makes the experience much more memorable. An individual is much more likely to remember an emotionally charged interaction than one that is muted and devoid of emotions. And we do want the individual to remember the appropriate response that produced the reinforcement. This facilitates learning on an experiential and biological level. It has a deeper and longer-lasting effect on the individual.

Rapport

To develop a good working relationship, one must build a rapport between themselves and the clients they serve. Building rapport can be achieved in many ways, all of which lock in on the individual's needs and preferences whose trust you want to earn. If the individual you are attempting to build a rapport with loves classical music, you should discuss, ask about, or put on classical music for them. If they are a vegetarian and don't like to eat meat for health reasons or humanitarian reasons, you can discuss that and show interest in how one becomes a vegetarian. Creating rapport is about connecting with the other person. Thus, anything that you see in them that you can relate to, do so by telling them about it or bringing it up in your conversation. The idea is to have the client feel like you are a lot like them by focusing on things that you are truly interested in. This will lead to trust, and trust will lead to a greater possibility of them following your advice and behavior plan in the future if it is perceived as sincere. I have found that even very low-functioning individuals can tell when you are not sincere.

The most powerful way to create rapport, especially with nonverbal people, is to anticipate their needs and facilitate the meeting of those needs. For example, when it gets hot while outside with your client and you can see that they are perspiring, you can go to them and ask them if they would like a nice cold drink. If they show you in some way that they would, or even if they can't, bring them the drink and let them know that they looked like they could use it. Also, moving them to a cool shaded area would be just as good, or spraying them with a soft mist of cool water, or just putting a cold towel to wipe their face. Anything that will make the individual feel more comfortable will promote rapport. More superficial ways also work, such as the dentist giving out lollipops or having nonstop cartoons running in their waiting room. Pandering to people's emotions creates a sense of belonging that is safe. When one feels safe, they are much more likely to try new things or endure things that are a little uncomfortable.

A word must be said about authenticity. Often, people can see right through superficial attempts at currying favor. Thus, it is always better to talk and deal with issues that you are sincere about than trying to pretend you know something that you don't. If you don't know anything about what the other person likes, you can genuinely ask to be enlightened about that subject rather than pretend you know something about it. Because sooner or later, you will say or do something that will reveal to the other person that you are faking it. This is very detrimental to the rapport you have already built and definitely not good for any future rapport that you are trying to build. Nonverbal people are much more in tune with signs of emotions than the words that are spoken. So you have to be very careful not to be too superficial or putting it on to build that rapport when dealing with such people. Honesty is the best policy in this situation. When an individual does not speak, and is mentally challenged, they are not attending to your speech but, rather, to you body language. They assess who you are based totally on your attitude and what you project in the situation. A receptive, inquisitive, but cheerful attitude not only seems best in new situations, but also works in any situation. Not being too serious or forceful in your opinions and attitude is the best approach when dealing with someone who may already know that you are there to fix them. In many cases, they are fearful, anxious, and unwilling to open up to you. It takes a very happy and flexible outlook to win someone like that over. And for some others, nothing will work, and they will throw things at you. In that case, you will have to obtain all necessary information from the others around the person, whether it is family members, instructors, or direct care staff.

The last point to make about building a rapport is the principle of reciprocity mentioned earlier. Make sure that in your interaction with the client, you adjust your own behavior to their behavior. For example, if you approach them and they make an effort to get away from you, back off and apologize for upsetting them or encroaching on their territory. If later you see them peering out at you from behind a wall, invite them to join you. Remain flexible and ready to take the interaction wherever it goes without getting emotional about it. Remember, you are entering into their space. Even if they are in your office, you are still trying to pry into their personal life and know what they do in their private lives. Never assume that they don't understand or don't know what's going on. Many seemingly very low-functioning clients can surprise you as to what they know about you and your function in relation to them.

Choosing Reinforcers

The *first* thing you should think about is that the best reinforcer is going to be the one that best meets the individual's needs. Thus, the best possible scenario is to teach the individual to meet their own need, thus giving them the ability to reinforce themselves. Now if this is true, which it is, then it follows that any reinforcer will not be a reinforcer all of the time since needs are constantly changing. So the *second* thing one must keep in mind is to have more than one reinforcer in relation to any individual so that you can also avoid the satiation effect mentioned earlier. There are only so many M&M'S one can eat! The *third* thing to keep in mind is availability and immediacy by which you can administer that reinforcer. It must be available at all times and given right when the behavior occurs, if possible. And lastly, try to have a natural reinforcer that is related to the behavior you want to change when possible. An example of this would consist of going on a walk once the individual can successfully dress themselves. Or eating a treat once you participate in making it. Note the difference between that and having someone earn a soda for making their bed. Earning a soda has nothing to do with making a bed. So that would not be a natural reinforcer. Sometimes natural reinforcers are not possible, and thus, we will use secondary reinforcers.

Due to these three issues, it is a good idea to consider a secondary reinforcer since you can use just about anything—tokens, chips, beans, or even just a check mark on a card. It would be appropriate here to explain the difference between a *primary reinforcer* and a *secondary reinforcer*. A primary reinforcer is a reinforcer that is directly experienced, such as food, soda, a walk in the park. A secondary reinforcer is one that can lead you to the primary reinforcer, such as money. You can buy M&M'S with money, but you cannot eat the money directly. That is why it is called a secondary reinforcer because it is not a reinforcer in and of itself, but only because it can be used to obtain the actual reinforcer, which is the primary reinforcer.

In addition to the above-noted parameters, you also have to keep in mind the schedule that you will use, how often they will earn what you are offering, and how feasible it is for the current situation you are in. For example, a very obese person should not be rewarded frequently with food. However, since food is very reinforcing for such a person, they could earn an ice cream or a slice of pizza if they are able to demonstrate a weight loss, for example. Thus, choosing a reinforcer will depend on many things. The important thing to keep in mind is that the goal is to remove the reinforcer once the behavior therapy has been completed. That is why natural reinforcers are preferable, because they will be there indefinitely, and we don't have to worry about fading them out. Artificial reinforcers must be eventually faded out unless they are so prevalent in the environment that they can continue to be used.

My personal preference is the natural approach that is based on needs. Thus, if an individual is having behavioral problems, which are largely communication problems as I have explained earlier, then the best outcome would be to teach that individual to effectively express their need, or, better yet, teach them how to go about meeting their own needs. I was at a residential facility once early in the morning, and all of the residents except for one had already left for day program. The only staff there excused herself to go to the restroom, leaving me alone with the remaining resident that I have never met and know nothing about. This resident was physically much bigger than me and ambulatory. I was standing in the kitchen, and he was a few feet away in the dining room. As I looked at him, he came straight at me, pushed me to the side, opened the cupboard, grabbed a can of coffee, opened it, and proceeded to drink the coffee flakes. I immediately stopped him using physical prompts in fear that he will choke himself and asked him if he wanted to have some coffee. He was nonverbal but stopped and kept looking at me. I assumed I was correct and told him that you have to make the coffee first. I then proceeded to walk him through the process of getting the filter, putting the coffee flakes in it and putting the filter back into the machine, obtaining the water, pouring it in, and turning the machine on. What I did not know is that I was there to evaluate him for his violent behavior of going after coffee. Without my knowledge, I had already developed and implemented the behavior plan that was effective in dealing with that behavior. However, if I had not seen the behavior directly, I would have been puzzled if staff did not describe it as I saw it. I was simply informed that he gets violent about going in the kitchen and grabbing things, so the rule of the house was to keep him out of the kitchen. Once the plan was in place, he had no problems at all with going in the kitchen and waiting to make the coffee. He was an addict! I suppose that I was effective only because it happened to be early in the morning and I was thinking the same thing, to get some coffee.

I believe that all behaviors stem from a problem in communication and are provoked by unmet needs.

The best reinforcer, then, is the item, thing, or event that meets the need of the person whose behavior we want to change at that moment in time. This is why I spent some time earlier talking about needs, nonverbal communication, emotions, etc., because even with those who can talk, they are not always good communicators. So one has to go beyond the obvious and what is said and look at the bigger picture. Although what I am about to say is *so not* scientific, I do use it frequently. I simply ask myself these questions: Why would I do what this person is doing? What feeling, emotion, or need would lead me to exhibit this behavior? I do this because in working with very involved individuals, I find that we are not that different after all. Developmentally disabled people or handicapped individuals do not come from Planet X! They have similar needs, and similar ways of attempting to procure those needs. The reason why they often seem so foreign to us is that the primary way of doing anything in our society rests on proper and appropriate communication skills. Try to get through the day without saying a word to anyone, and you will quickly find that you cannot make it for a couple of hours without the need to say something.

CHAPTER 10

Behavior Intervention

Be the Example

Whatever your behavior plan prescribes, it must be congruent with the behavior of those who deal with and take care of the person whose behavior you want to change. Thus, you cannot put someone on a soda diet where they get soda only during meals while the staff are walking around all day with sodas in their hands. Thus, the first thing that you have to be cognizant of is the behavior of those that will carry out the behavior plan and what interventions are possible within the environment that the person is in. The tendency to do as you see rather than what you hear is very much part of our physiology. The phrase "monkey see, monkey do" has some actual neurological basis to it on the human level. Dr. Daniel J. Siegel describes this in his *The Mindful Brain*: "Mirror properties in the nervous system are essentially defined as the ways in which our social brain has processes in which it perceives the intentional, goal-directed actions of others and links this perception to the priming of the motor systems to engage in that same action" Siegel, D. J. (2007). *The mindful brain: Reflection and attunement in the cultivation of well-being*, W. W. Norton & Company, Inc. New York, New York. What this means is that we have neurological structures that are ready to mimic whatever we see. So no matter what the behavioral plan and what you want the individual to do, this will be overridden by the behaviors being displayed in front of them. Hence the need to be the example. Do not require the client to do what others around them will not do. If this is what has to happen, then you must include in your plan a way to shield them

134

from those other individuals who will be engaging in the target behavior you want to eradicate.

One of the best tricks I learned in teaching hyperactive children in an SLDA (severe language developmental aphasia) class was to start whispering when they were all loud and running around screaming. As I continued to whisper, the room became quieter and quieter trying to hear what I was saying. Then if I were to ask a question, they would answer me with a whisper. This tendency to do what others do is what drives most of learning in the normal population. It is only when you start working with challenged individuals that you find how much they are missing by not being able to simply watch and mimic others. For those individuals, the process has to be more structured, more repetitive, and prompted. This is why I stated earlier that we tend to do the opposite of what we should do with the developmentally disabled, which is to do more and not less training.

The Plan

Obviously, I cannot write a plan for you that will deal with all possible behaviors, but what I will attempt to do is provide you with the structure of the plan and what it should address. In general, I view behavioral problems as inappropriate communications of needs. Thus, in doing the functional analysis, one should pay close attention to this aspect of the person they are dealing with. A functional analysis, on many occasions, demonstrates that the function of the behavior is to call attention to oneself. The reason for needing that attention is what you should focus on. Once that has been discovered, the plan becomes obvious in the sense that you will be developing a plan that will meet that need for the individual, without exhibiting the inappropriate behavior but, rather, by exhibiting the replacement behavior. The general structure I use is one that has three parts:

- a plan to prevent
- a plan to teach a more appropriate response
- a plan to deal with the behavior to discourage its reoccurrence

I will give a general example of each one below.

The Plan to Prevent

The plan to prevent should consist of avoiding those tasks, events, or places that provoke the behavior. Thus, if the person you are dealing with does not like loud and noisy places, you avoid subjecting them to those places until they are trained to deal with such stimulation through the next two steps in the plan. If you have to take them to a place like that, you should have an exit strategy ready in case they have a serious problem. This would consist not only of where you will take them, but also if there are enough people to supervise and redirect the behavior away from the loud and noisy place. Thus, you would position them toward the fringes of the place, close to the doors or exits to leave, so that if they begin to get uncomfortable, they can easily leave the place quickly.

If it is an individual who is a picky eater and will have a tantrum when required to eat foods they do not like, always provide them with choices of things to eat.

If it is a person who refuses to mop the floor for any reason, give them a different task, and do not require them to mop the floor.

If it is a person who does not tolerate the intense stimulation of a shower, provide them with the opportunity to take a bath instead.

The Plan to Teach

In this section, you want to outline how you are going to teach this individual to either avoid or tolerate the antecedent that provokes the behavior. So for the individual who does not like loud, noisy places, we will attempt to teach two things: how to tolerate through systematic desensitization and how to escape or avoid the activity by verbalizing that they do not want to go, or how to tell you they need to leave once there. Again, as mentioned above when I was explaining this plan through ergonomics, the interventionist must keep a close watch on the person to make sure to intervene as soon as there are any signs of discomfort. If you wait too long and the behavior occurs, learning must then be achieved through negative means by the consequence, which is not the best way to learn. The plan to teach is always about training the individual to deal with a source of stimulation they do not like. It is training in appropriate avoidance behavior, like saying "No, thank you!" in whatever capacity the individual has at their disposal. Thus, it is not always a verbal response, but could be a sign or gesture.

The plan to teach should also concern itself with tolerance. Even if one avoids taking the person to loud and noisy places, there may be a time, such as during a fire drill, that they will have to cope with loud and noisy environments. Thus, training in tolerance would be quite useful to the individual. The way to do this would be to simply expose them to the loud and noisy environment in small doses and give them an incentive to increase the time that they are there, such as going to McDonald's right after the experience or whatever place they like. This time will be slowly increased, but terminated at the first signs of discomfort, until they can be there for a substantial amount of time. It would help if you find an activity or preferred item that can be purchased or done there at the loud and noisy place to give additional incentives to be there.

The Plan to Intervene

The plan to intervene with the behavior once it occurs is the most negative aspect of the whole plan. If you get to that point, it means that the two previous strategies have not worked as well as we had hoped. It may be because you have not been observant enough to the antecedents and missed some signs that the individual was having a problem. Or it may be that the intensity of the situation quickly overwhelmed the individual and they had no time to exhibit antecedent behaviors. Whatever the cause, the problem now is that almost anything you do will be at least partially reinforcing since it will change the situation in such a way as to provide the escape that they are looking for. Thus, to stay true to behavioral principles, we cannot do anything that would be deemed reinforcing for the individual for fear of propagating the behavior. So if we remain with the same example of a person not wanting to be in the noisy and crowded mall, we must *not* allow them to leave the mall until they calm down or at least stop the screaming and flailing around long enough to give us the appropriate response such as saying it is too loud, stating that they want to leave, or simply making the sign for *break* or *too loud*. Ergonomically, they will engage in the behavior longer, burning more energy, and there is no benefit because they will not escape. But as soon as they exhibit the appropriate response, escape should come quickly and without delay. Because learning occurs the fastest when the stimulus and response immediately follow each other. Thus, we do not want escape to follow tantrums. We want escape to result from making the appropriate response.

All intervention plans should follow the same logic—to ignore and prevent escape when the inappropriate behavior occurs and attend to and immediately act on the appropriate response. It is not cheating to give the individual the appropriate response and have them repeat it. The point is to have them experience making the response and achieving escape as a result of making that response. Again, learning is not the same as the accumulation of information. Learning is a result of experience. So no matter what you tell your children, they will behave more like you behave and not like you say they should behave.

This is all I want to say about structuring a plan. All plans must be shaped around the person who will be the recipient of it as well as the behavior we are attempting to eradicate. This chapter is perhaps the shortest one since many of these points have been made in previous chapters. I simply provided a structure into which one can place these various aspects of behavior change. Behavior change is much more an art form than it is a science. The interventionist must know when to insist on performance and when to back off, depending on the emotional state of the individual whose behavior we want to change. Again, happiness is the key. If a person is happy, they are not inclined to give you a hard time. To make people happy, their needs must be met. Their needs can be met only if they know how to meet their own needs. If they are unable to do so, it places the burden on the interventionist, first to know what the need is, then to teach the individual how to meet it. This is the global aspect of the behavior change that I would like now to turn to.

CHAPTER 11

The Target Population

The usual target population that is the recipient of the methods of applied behavior analysis consists largely of the handicapped, developmentally disabled population, or children having behavioral problems in schools. Currently, autism seems to be the focus of much of the behavioral work, and many behavior analysts cater to this group. However, this group is quite varied, and the methods employed are quite diverse. There is also a wide range of settings in which one may receive behavioral services. It is beyond the scope of this chapter to cover all of these options, but the main focus will simply be on the general target population and their behavioral problems.

Autism

The autistic population, as I mentioned, is very much the focus of many behavioral venues at the current time (2009). One of the reasons for such an accelerated rate of interest in this group may be the range of autistic individuals that can be labeled as such under the new designation of the autism spectrum disorders, which covers individuals that are low functioning and nonverbal to very high functioning and verbal—Asperger's syndrome representing the very high end of autism and Rhett syndrome representing the low end. As the definition widens, so does the number of cases that can be counted. Estimates of occurrences have been as high as six in every one thousand children will be affected by autism.

As a practitioner in the field, it appears to me that there is always a disease of the month every few years. A few years ago, it was attention deficit hyperactivity disorder (ADHD), and now it appears to be autism spectrum disorder (ASD). We have to be careful about what label we place on children because what we designate them to be will determine the services and level of those services that they will be able to receive. There is a great deal of overlap between autism and ADHD, as well as autism and Down syndrome. The danger is that once we label a person, we tend to treat them based on the class of individuals labeled as such and not necessarily treating them as the individuals that they are. Granted, these labels are necessary and convenient in terms of placement and service issues, but let us not forget that they still remain individuals.

The important point to remember is that regardless of what diagnosis the individual has, it should not automatically follow that they should receive one treatment as opposed to another. Each individual is a unique set of genetic material, reinforcement history, biological stamina, and background; and each individual will have their own needs and preferences that will dictate how best they are able to learn the required skills to survive. Again, as a practitioner, I believe the diagnosis is secondary to the degree of response I get from my patients in relation to what I do in treatment. Thus, understanding the diagnosis is not nearly as important as understanding the individual you are treating. Knowing what they like and what they don't like is more important in behavior therapy than if they are high or low functioning and whether they have ADHD or ASD or both. What is great about behavior therapy is that it does not change its basic principles of operation no matter what the target population is.

One of the unique aspects of the autistic population is the frequency at which they operate. If you could for a moment visualize the human organism as a biological entity that emanates energy, you can quickly see that some individuals are low-energy individuals and some are higher-energy individuals. The higher the energy, the more intense the individual is. Behaviorally, the way these gradient levels of energy are expressed are in the volume of the voice, the quickness of behavioral movements, the speed of speech or execution of a task, and, most revealing yet the least quantifiable, the look in their eyes, which tends to be very attentive and scanning the environment much more carefully than lower-energy individuals. In relation to these parameters, I place autistic people at the higher end of the energy scale than normal individuals and other classified mentally retarded people below the normal level of excitation. This parameter is primarily one that is controlled by the central nervous system. It is volume or speed at which that particular person vibrates or functions. It would be interesting to measure the amount of energy being emitted from these different populations to see if this theory is correct. I am concluding the order based on my personal experience with a wide variety of developmentally disabled people, from the extremely low functioning that cannot do anything for themselves to those that work at Pizza Hut and ride the bus home to their own apartments.

It is this energy field that I believe to be the basis for Kirlian photography or the aura that some see before a patient is about to have a seizure. I also believe that it is visual to dogs who can be trained to detect it prior to the seizure and actually lead their masters to a place to sit or lie down prior to the occurrence of the seizure. So in closing this discussion before sounding like I am proselytizing some sort of religion, I believe that autistic people tend to have a more intense or higher frequency at which they operate, and a good approach to use with them in general is one that can calm that intensity to facilitate learning and focusing.

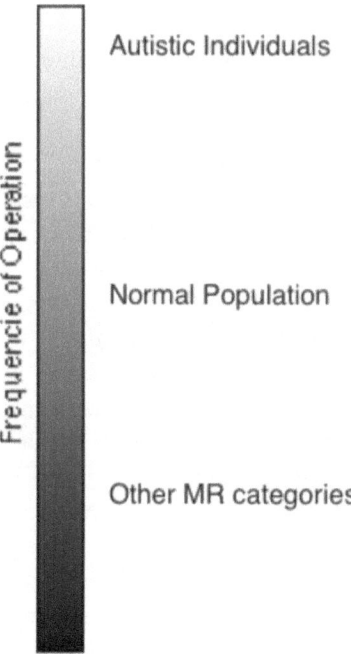

The last word I would like to state before moving away from autism is this—no matter what anyone tells you, there is no cure for autism! The reason why there is no cure is because we do not know why autism happens. Once we find out the mechanism of action that results in an autistic child, we may be able to focus on changing that condition and thereby cure autism. But until then, the focus should remain on treatments that we know work, namely, applied behavior analysis.

Areas of Concern

The target population in need of behavioral services are usually individuals that are *cognitively, socially,* and *communicatively* impaired. Thus, whether they have autism, Down syndrome, or ADHD—to name a few of the popularly known disorders among the hundreds that we have discovered—they will invariably have deficits in those three areas. Applied behavioral analysis, then, becomes the primary tool to remedy the imbalances in those three parameters of the human experience. In earlier chapters, I have already discussed the communication arena, which will also significantly affect the social domain. However, the most significant barrier to progress is the cognitive domain, which is often ignored in applied behavior analysis programs. I want to again remind the reader of the revenge case described earlier, where a behavior plan was no longer necessary once the client believed the problem was more effectively resolved using my suggestion of reporting on the other client to get his revenge instead of assaulting him. This is called *cognitive restructuring*. The patient has effectively rearranged his thought patterns to understand a particular emotion in such a way as to affect the behavior he will engage in when he experiences that emotion again in the future. Once the restructuring occurs, the behavior problem no longer exists. The problem with this approach is that it can only work with the higher-functioning and verbal clients, who are a minority of my caseload. However, no matter what the syndrome we are working with, each syndrome has individuals within that group that are high and low functioning, and verbal to nonverbal. Again, the gradient effect is in operation here as it is in every aspect of the human experience. So there are degrees of effectiveness in any of the parameters that are affected, and there is no set procedure that applies to all cases. So let's examine these three areas, how they manifest themselves, and how they can be approached.

The Cognitive Domain

By definition, anyone who is classified as mentally retarded has an impaired cognition in reference to the norm. What is meant by that is that the individual is unable to utilize the general principles of reasoning, has difficulty with abstractions, and is unable to see the big picture. As a result, moral development is almost completely missing. Right and wrong are more things that they have memorized from others and mean they will or will not gain reinforcement if they do or do not do things labeled right or wrong. Morality is a concrete aspect of their behavior, and philosophy has little to do with it. So I will not hit Johnny not because it is morally wrong to hit others because it will make them hurt and they don't deserve that from you, but because I won't earn my soda if I do it. So the cognitive domain manifests itself in seemingly selfish behavior, where the individual is seeking to satisfy only themselves at the expense of others. However, this is an unfair characterization of the behavior and has moral tones to it that do not apply. It is not selfish to do something that only applies to you when all you know how to control is yourself and even that assumption is only partly true. The more that one is affected by their own situation, the less they are able to worry about yours. Thus, many severely challenged individuals are unable to think about or empathize with others because they are too busy attempting to think about and empathizing about their own situation.

The implication for treatment is an obvious one if the preceding paragraph is correct. One cannot use cognitive reasoning or moral verbal restructuring as much as they should be using behaviorally based practices that emphasize the outcomes and consequences of their actions. Thus, when an individual hits another, moral verbalizations about how wrong it is to hit people, or that it is not nice, are not as effective as stating that when you hit others, they don't like it and they won't play with you or share their toys with you when you do that. And given that most developmentally disabled individuals, especially autistic individuals, are affected by anxiety due to the fact that they are not in control of their own lives, giving them verbal prompts like "We will have coffee later" is inappropriate since later can be any time, and this type of response will simply provoke perseveration of continuously asking if it is time to get coffee. It is better to provide them with some anchor or time marker to hang on to, such as, "We will have coffee right after we finish our lunch."

The Social Domain

The social domain is quite vexing for handicapped people. You never know how much you depend on other people's cooperation until you are handicapped in some way. I once was involved in a motorcycle accident and was not very hurt. However, I had scraped one of my feet quite badly and could not put shoes on it for approximately six to eight weeks. That simple disability changed how I live my life. My routines all had to change, and relying on others was much more prevalent in my daily dealings with the environment. You realize that we are all in competition for the same resources; and if you are not fit enough to get into that line, or be somewhere on time, others will quickly take your turn and cast you aside. You find how nice some people can be and how selfish most people are. Our society, as it has evolved, assumes an intact organism that can maneuver around obstacles that appear to be everywhere once you are disabled. If not for certain ramps and elevators, many places are still out of reach for the disabled. This is why we passed the Disability Act in California to make sure that all business locations are accessible to the handicapped.

Meeting our needs necessitates interaction with the social structure. So if you are physically handicapped but are able to speak, you can ask others to help, and usually there is no problem getting around obstacles. However, if you are handicapped in speech but are physically OK, you are actually more disabled than someone in a wheelchair that can speak because no one knows, understands, or cares about what you want or need. Almost 90 percent of all social interaction is verbal. So if you can't talk, you are almost totally disabled in the social domain and are at a greater disadvantage than someone who is physically disabled but able to speak.

The implication for treatment in this area will have to focus on, first and foremost, not engaging in behaviors that are offensive to others. This would include obvious things like not masturbating in public, not urinating in public, not picking your nose, saying excuse me after burping or passing gas, and not taking your clothes off because they bother you. Once you teach those basic skills, you must advance to the more subtle mannerisms such as not standing too close to others, not hugging everyone you see, not getting in front of others to be served, waiting your turn, asking for things rather than just taking things, and not pushing others to get them out of the way. These are all skills that must be taught before we even get to the communication part of the training, where you ask for help, are able to dial your home phone number in case you get lost, etc., so that you can be safe in the community even if your caretaker loses you. For example, if a person gets lost and does not know where they are, they should have a card with them that has information about their place of residence, their phone number, and their disability clearly stated. Training will consist of showing that card to someone, hopefully a police officer, once the individual gets lost.

We can argue that all intervention plans are, in one way or another, teaching more appropriate social behavior to meet one's needs and preferences. The social domain is one of the major casualties of being developmentally disabled. When one is disabled and cannot get around or does not know how to get around, their social world is much smaller than that of the nonhandicapped individual. And this is why residential placement, in many ways, is much more beneficial to a developmentally disabled person than staying home with their own families. If the individual in question is the only one that is disabled in the house, they will have no peer group to relate to. Within the residential environment, at least the individual is around other individuals with similar needs and interests, and all activities are designed around those disabilities. This is usually not the case at their own family's home. Parents often wait too long to place their children, believing the best place for them is home. I am sure for many cases that is true whereas in other cases it is not. However, I would like to point out that in most cases, a developmentally disabled individual will wind up in residential care. And the longer they stay away from that option and the later they enter into residential living, the harder it will be for them to adjust and the older their parents will be. This sets into motion an urgency that sometimes leads to inappropriate placements. My suggestion is to look for residential placement early until a good program is found, place the child at that time while you are still young enough to monitor their progress, take them home on a regular basis to keep the family their life, or place them on a waiting list if no openings are available. In this way, you have plenty of time to take them out and try some other home if the one you chose was not what you had hoped for. In many of the residential homes I serve, the individuals enjoy going home to see their families, but many are eager to come back to their own home in the residential placement environment with their friends and peers.

The Communication Domain

I will not repeat myself about the importance of communication since I have discussed this issue in several places already. However, I will simply deal with the options available that one can look into to improve the communicable ability of someone that is handicapped.

The first choice to look into, which would be the least restrictive alternative, would be to develop and/or improve speech. This is the most common way that most people use to communicate. However, it is not the only one. When that option is not available, the next best thing would be total communication training, which consists of every means possible with the exception of special devices to communicate needs. This would include vocal sounds, pointing, gesturing, or taking the person by the hand and leading them to the object or thing they want. This approach can also make use of formal sign language words, phrases, or the alphabet to spell out words.

When these minimally invasive techniques are not enough, speech aids can be employed. This may be as simple as having a sign that has Yes and No on it attached to a key chain with lots of pictures on it, all the way to sophisticated computers that will speak for you when you hit the right button. There is no right answer as to what will work. An exhaustive assessment needs to be made of the individual and a solution developed around their disability as well as their preference. This process of improving communication skills is something that continues for most of their life and should be part of most intervention plans.

CHAPTER 12

A View from the Other Side

The Human Touch

The best information one can have to be an effective behavior change agent is to know as much as possible about the person you are trying to create the change in. I have found that one of the most useful and fruitful avenues for accumulating such knowledge is simply to imagine oneself being the person you are trying to change. By this I mean to experience their particular situation and asking ourselves what would cause us to behave in this manner. Understanding the experience of the other can provide us with very valuable information as to what their needs are and how to avoid a behavioral outburst with them.

For example, a staff member comes to the residential facility to start their shift. They walk in, residents are sitting around in the living room watching television. The staff person walks toward another staff person and begins talking to them for a good fifteen to twenty minutes. Mainly, the staff just starting the shift is getting information from the one finishing up her shift as to how things are going and what she needs to do on this day. After putting some laundry away, taking a phone call, and talking to another staff member again—but this time about her phone call—she turns to one of the residents and proceeds to shower them. The resident is uncooperative and resistive to her efforts and physically refuses to go. The staff member is baffled and asks another staff member if this particular resident is having problems. The response is a negative. The resident has not been exhibiting behavioral problems, and nothing happened recently to upset them. So the staff assumes that the resident is in a bad mood. She leaves them alone, and she'll attempt to give them their shower at a later time.

Now let's view this exactly same situation from the resident's point of view. So I am sitting in my house, watching television; my staff—the one I will have to depend on to help me bathe, eat, and get ready for bed later—comes into the house. She passes right by me and doesn't even acknowledge that I exist, then goes to talk to another staff for a very long time. It is a very long time because I am waiting for her to acknowledge me because today is movie night and I wanted her to ask me what I want so that I can tell her I want to watch *Grease* again. I keep looking over there, and she is still ignoring me. OK now, she is finished talking to the other staff; maybe she will come over and ask me now. Oh no, she is doing laundry. Why doesn't she come over here and ask me about the movie? Oh now, she is on the phone. She is going outside. Is she coming back, or did she have to leave? Am I going to see a movie tonight? Where is she? OK, here she comes. I'll tell her about the movie when she asks me. Do what? Take a shower? What about my movie? No, I am not going to go. I want to talk about the movie. Stop trying to get me to go take a shower. I don't care about the shower. I want to watch *Grease!*

This scenario is quite common in most residential facilities. Staff will usually focus so much on their job and their agenda and other coworkers that they forget they are in somebody else's house—someone who depends on them to do for them the things that they cannot do for themselves. And you come in, ignore them as if they don't matter, and go talk to your friend like you own the place; and the only time you have anything to say to me is when you're telling me what to do. So I am uncooperative because I am trying to communicate to you that I am upset with you. Since I cannot talk, I depend on you to ask me, like you did last week. Why didn't you ask me this week? Did I do something wrong?

Beware of Your Agenda

The point is that many staff focus too much on their own agenda and not enough on the agenda of their residents. From the residents' point of view, they have no agenda other than what they are feeling at that moment. Yet we act like they are being difficult when they don't simply follow our agenda and do what we ask them to do, as if there is an obvious logic to this sort of thinking. But why would they have any idea as to what our agenda is and why should they follow it? It is up to us to compensate for this lack of reciprocity in communication. After all, we are the paid staff in charge of providing care; the resident is not. When staff are exclusively concerned with their agenda and neglect to pay attention to behavioral antecedents such as noncompliance and resistiveness, the problem will only escalate if not dealt with effectively, usually in the form of one-on-one attention from staff. The longer you wait to intervene, the longer it will take to calm them down. So the earlier the intervention, the more effective it will be. Thus, if you focus on your agenda and don't pay attention to save time, you will lose more time by having to deal with a bigger and more intense behavioral episode.

There are a lot of ideas out there concerning what is the best way to program and engage the developmentally disabled population into our society so that they do all of those things that we do. There is an assumption that they all would like to be productive, independent, and like us. There is a fundamental flaw in this logic, namely, that we don't all like the same thing and some normal people would not like to be like most people with a regular job, a place to stay, and a stable social network. Some people live radically different lives. Personal preferences are unique to each individual whether they are developmentally disabled or not. Thus, we should not treat each new innovation in programming as "thee" answer to the developmentally disabled population. Every approach has some validity with some segment of the population. Thus, each new innovation should be added to our arsenal of tools to help this population, but not attempt to impose each new approach to all individuals.

The Fallacy of Integration

A case in point will illustrate the strength and weakness of programs and why all programs should be considered and none excluded. In the old days, approximately twenty years ago, sheltered workshops were state-of-the-art programming for the developmentally disabled. However, as volunteer work, supported employment and competitive employment developed and were made available, sheltered workshops were viewed as passé. It became considered as a more restrictive placement than community-based employment. So pressure was brought to bear on many clients who were in sheltered workshops but had the potential for competitive employment. One of my clients was a high-functioning individual that was the equivalent of a foreman on the warehouse floor in a sheltered workshop. He was considered for competitive employment, and they got him a job at McDonnell's. This individual took the bus from his residential placement to McDonnell's and returned home the same way without any supervision. After almost two years, he began having problems. Staff was reporting about him coming to work late, returning late from lunch, and generally having a bad attitude. He was referred to me for a solution since he's been my client for years. After interviewing him, it became apparent that after almost two years of doing a good job at McDonnell's, they were still treating him like someone lower than them, would not socialize with him, and while they would go to lunch together, they would not invite him. When I asked him what he would like to see happen, he simply stated that he wanted to be back at the sheltered workshop with his friends. It turned out that he would rather be a big fish in a small pond than a small fish in a big pond.

Hopefully, you are not interpreting the previous paragraph as an indictment on supported or competitive employment. The only point I was trying to make is that both jobs had something to offer that was valuable, but his needs changed, and he was missing his friends more than getting reinforcement from the money and independence, which he did like at first. He's been back at the sheltered workshop now for six years and does not want to change.

The scenario I describe above has played out several times in different situations and with different functional levels. The fact of the matter is that regardless of how well a developmentally disabled individual can perform a task or do a job for an employer, if the setting does not provide an atmosphere of acceptance, it will be difficult to keep the client there. Again, the tangible rewards are not the true motivators. Although they are the most obvious, they were not the strongest reinforcer for the client described above.

His relationship with his peers was much more important. This illustrates how our perceptions are biased by our own values, and we assume that the same is true for our clients.

The False Economy

From the point of view of the client or resident, they are asked to do a variety of things that make no sense to them. The reason why that is consists of the fact that they live in a false economy. The two most powerful reinforcers for the general population—namely sex and money—are largely denied the developmentally disabled population. Most of us are motivated by these two things: one, sex, we are motivated by through genetics; and the other, money, we are motivated by because we cannot meet our needs without it. However, for a developmentally disabled person, money becomes irrelevant since their rent and all other expenses are paid for them, thus removing one of the most significant motivators to achieve and produce in our culture. As for sex, most of my clients are living in same-sex homes; either they are all males or females. Those facilities that have mixed population usually consist of four men and two women since it appears that there are more males affected. So even in those homes, there isn't a lot of choice or interaction since sexual interaction is usually discouraged, or at least not promoted due to the complications that could arise as a result of that type of behavior. Thus, the developmentally disabled individuals are rarely motivated by the things most important to our culture; yet we spend most of our efforts programming them to do the things that we do, not even considering the fact that many of us normal people would not work if we didn't have to. In essence, we are asking them to be like us, but their situation is so different than ours in reference to the motivational aspect of the human condition that the same parameters do not apply. Many are not even interested in sex. And you can see and observe how this is manifested by observing how they dress and groom themselves. In most cases, we have to teach individuals to be clean and neat, comb their hair, and make sure to brush their teeth and use deodorant. If attracting others is not on your mind and not part of your motivation, you will not spend a lot of time trying to look attractive.

Given the situation just described, it is unreasonable to expect our developmentally disabled population to be motivated like us concerning money and grooming. The reasons most of my clients enjoy working and producing are to impress those who take care of them, the social interactions they gain while at work, and the feeling that they are just like normal people. But you can see that if that reinforcement is not there, they also lose interest in the job without regard for the money or how rare good jobs are. I would argue that most of their motivation is social and not monetary. I literally cannot tell you how many times I have heard staff complain that the developmentally disabled person they are monitoring has the potential to do much more if only they would stop socializing and focus more on working. But again, why should they? They really don't understand how expensive it is to live, they have no appreciation for what it would actually take for them to be independent, and they don't gain or lose that much whether they work or not. Sometimes the only way they can relate to increasing their own production is if they want to go to Las Vegas or a cruise or something like that, then you see a temporary improvement in motivation to produce; but this motivation goes right back down as soon as they earn what they were aiming for.

Current Trends

The current environment expects all of these developmentally disabled individuals to integrate into normal society, independently travel to and from work, live in their own apartments, and make their own decisions. This sounds great until these illusions are tested in the real world. Granted, I have had minor successes in this area, but the failures have been much more frequent. In many ways, we are attempting to stick a square peg in a round hole. We are making outrageous assumptions about this population that are taken as obvious facts. Yet there is absolutely no data to prove these assertions. While I do believe that developmentally disabled people are very much like us in reference to human needs, they are not at all like us when it comes to their motivational base. As mentioned above, the two most powerful motivators in the world of the normals are sex and money, which play only a minor role in most developmentally disabled people.

Things are not always what they seem. For example, most people believe that the child or young adult is better off at home than in residential care. The opposite is actually true if the individual is placed in a home that is functioning as it should, meaning that it has the resources and philosophy that is supportive of their needs. Because the child or young adult will have a peer group that he relates to instead of being the only retarded individual in the family. In many ways, this is what we do when we are too aggressive in pushing these people into the community, namely, setting them up for failure by making them the only disabled person in the environment we put them in. Done correctly, this sort of integration can work if the appropriate supports are there. The only problem is that supports are only temporary. The assumption is, we will give them all the support they need to learn the job and the route to and from the job, then start removing the supports. This is where things get messy. Many of my clients can do everything asked of them so long as they are supervised. As soon as that supervision is removed, the deterioration begins. The reason why this occurs is because, again, we are operating under false assumptions, namely, that the client wants to succeed and be independent and will be reinforced with a paycheck if she does the job well. However, her motivation is to please you! If I am correct in my assumption, then what we are doing is setting the person up to fail, because as they do better, you punish them with less approval and presence of the person they were trying to please. And as they improve, they are left alone more and more with the normal population, who, we hope, will like them and treat them like everyone else. And this is the biggest fallacy of all—that if the disabled person does everything right, they will be part of that group and will be treated like everyone else. This simply does not happen. If it does at all, it is a rarity. More often, what we observe is that they become the pet of the group. Everyone takes care of them, but do not actually socialize with them. Everyone loves them, but they don't invite them out to lunch. They like being around them, but they won't do things with them on the weekends. I would argue that yes, indeed, they are like us in this respect; and if you treated any normal person this way, they would not like it either. The fact of the matter is that they are like us concerning their human needs, not like us in every way. I don't go out to lunch with most people I work with, only with those that I like or have some business with that could be taken care of at lunch. On the weekends or on my time off, I get together with people I like that are like me in reference to common interests. A developmentally disabled person will usually not have common interests with many in the normal population, and they are not able to do what these other normal people do, like drive to be able to meet someone someplace or have money to spend or the freedom to stay out all night drinking and hanging out.

Thus, although the developmentally disabled population is a lot like us, they are very different in their social and emotional needs, and in reference to their resources and interests. I would argue that it is actually less restrictive to be around others that are like you than to be arbitrarily placed with a bunch of normal people. Doing so will simply accentuate their disability, not make them more normal.

Consider this: we live in a rapidly changing society where the costs for basic needs are rising, many have more than one job to make ends meet, education is becoming more and more expensive and loans harder to get, and the competition out there is torturous. Within that environment, people fail, lose their jobs, become homeless, and have nervous breakdowns and panic attacks. They take medications or get strung out on drugs, they lie, they steal from each other, but still they can't manage to get ahead. And I am only talking about the normal people. People with intact brains and coping mechanisms based on experience and education in that world. And now we are ready to hurl upon this lovely environment some developmentally disabled people that have few, if any, of these coping skills with the expectation of succeeding, given the right supports. This reminds me of the baseball player who breaks a leg running the bases and the coach tells him to walk it off!

While I do believe that the disabled population has the potential to integrate into society a lot more than they have in the past, this integration must be implemented case by case. The amount of supports required and the type of supports is different for each client. Too often I have seen supports withdrawn only to see the client fail; and of course, the blame will be on the client rather than on the program that removed the supports too quickly.

I have had many clients "graduate" to the level of competitive employment, only to fail within a couple of months. I find the current trend in day programs disturbing. I primarily work in the San Fernando Valley area, and the trend in some of the day programs is to be completely community based. While I see some merits to this approach, I see bigger flaws. For one thing, behavioral issues, which are of particular interest to me, are dealt with less effectively in the community. In an effort not to make a scene in public setting where they can throw you out, staff is almost always forced to reinforce inappropriate behaviors by letting things go to avoid escalating the situation. So many of my clients who go to such programs are being systematically eliminated. Thus, the idea is to succeed or leave. When a program makes a global decision to transition *all* of its clients to a new paradigm that they have not been involved in previously, they are doing so for their own benefit and *not* for the benefit of the clients they serve. One size does not fit all. This is why I have stated that all programs are relevant to some people, and no programs or approaches should be abandoned. Again, rather than taking each new innovation as the only way to program individuals, we should consider each new way as an additional method to reach and incorporate these people into the fabric of society, keeping in mind that our society can be a cold and harmful place.

CHAPTER 13

Global Behavior Intervention

Variety Is the Spice of Life

In dealing with developmentally disabled people, or even regular people with children that have behavioral problems, what you find is that staff or family members restrict the number of places they go with that child or person in the fear that they may act out. Again, this is doing the opposite of what should be done. A person who acts out a great deal does so when they are in the presence of a safe and predictable environment. We all tend to do this in one way or another. For example, if we've had a rough day, we wait till we are with our friends or family members to vent what incompetent nincompoops we have had to deal with all day and how we would love to just give them a piece of our mind. Behaviorally, developmentally disabled individuals are not that much different. They tend to act out more in safe environments. Although there are exceptions to this general principle, it is true that when exposed to novel environments, at least some of your attention and effort must go to taking in that environment, understanding it, visually examining it, etc., to come to terms with it. Thus, a behaviorally challenged individual will have less energy at their disposal for exhibiting behavioral problems in novel environments than they would in a familiar environment. Subjecting them to a variety of stimulating and different environments can usually work in your favor. Idle hands are the devil's workshop, as they say. So keeping behaviorally challenged individuals at home for fear that they may act out is actually asking for trouble unless the person we are talking about is one of those individuals who loves to engage in self-stimulatory activity and does not mind being left alone for hours on end. Although that particular type of individual would not be a bigger behavioral problem at home, they will spend more time engaging in self-stimulation there and withdraw deeper into their world—something we do not want to encourage. Thus, even for those individuals, getting out and being exposed to novel stimulation would be a good thing for them to know and find a variety of ways to be stimulated. This view of intervention rests on viewing the individual from what I would call a *behavioral sociobiological* view.

I know this has not been scientifically proven, but I deal with a great deal of low-functioning clients that have to take gastrointestinal medications for ulcers. It is well known that ulcers could be caused by stress, and boredom is a form of stress. Just ask my ninety-year-old mother who cannot get around on her own how nerve-racking boredom is to her. Here again, we tend to do the opposite of what we should be doing. Staff and parents are constantly assuming that low-functioning individuals, simply because they do not ask for anything, don't need anything. This assumption, I would bet, is absolutely not true. And if there was a way to prove it, I would bet that those individuals would benefit from stimulation of *any* kind, especially of being in novel places they have never seen or experienced, such as putting their feet in the water at a lake or the ocean or being out in the sun, in the rain, or by the pool under an umbrella.

How Much Variety Is Enough

Everyone has their own level of need concerning stimulation. Some of us need a lot, and some of us need a little. To gauge the level needed for any particular individual, one should pay attention to several physiological and behavioral patterns. For example, if the person in question has problems sleeping at night, this may be an indication that their day did not deplete their available energy enough to allow them to sleep. If they appear restless by engaging in repetitive movements, if they engage in a great deal of self-stimulatory activity, if they get constipated often, or if they seem unhappy in general, all mean that they are sensory deprived and could use some novel stimulation. And when I say novel stimulation, I don't mean going on a cruise to the Bahamas. It could be as simple as walking around the block once a day or going to the doughnut shop, the post office, or the bank. Stimulation is stimulation, regardless of what form it comes in. Thus, you want to gear the amount of stimulation you provide the person needing intervention in accordance to these symptoms as well as to their reaction when doing those things. In general, what I see as I go to many day programs, residential facilities, homes, and schools is a pattern of energy constipation. Being hyperactive from birth, I am quite sensitive to these issues. I had significant problems in school due to this lack of energy expenditure. Sure I played basketball, tennis, fencing, etc., but the majority of my time was sitting in class. I see this with many of my clients who appear to be restless, exhibiting symptoms I used to exhibit in the classroom. If only I had a dollar for every time a teacher told me to stop swinging my legs, to keep my hands quiet, I would be a millionaire right now and would not have to write a book to make money! So the bottom line concerning the amount of stimulation that the person needs is dependent on their reaction to what you provide and how many of the symptoms mentioned above are still being exhibited. Let me emphasize, the symptoms mentioned do not constitute a complete list. There may be many other ways that your particular client or child may exhibit boredom. All you can do is keep subjecting them to stimulation and watching how they react to it, not only during the stimulation, but also later on once they get home.

Happiness

As I have mentioned throughout many chapters of this book, happiness is the ultimate goal of all behavior. Another way to put it is that the goal is to be free from *all* discomfort. As demonstrated by the discussion on need states early in the book, biological organisms are constantly experiencing deficit states, which result in the experience of discomfort that must be met with responses to remedy the situation and bring the imbalance back to a balanced state. How effective we are in achieving this balance seems to be the key to happiness. But the situation is not quite that simple. For example, rich people who have the means to get anything they want are not necessarily happier than those who don't have those resources at their disposal. The trick is not to have everything you want, but to have what you need.

I heard a story once about a man who, in search for the ultimate truth, traveled many miles to find that truth. He heard of a particular guru who had the answer to this quest and was willing to give it to anyone who would visit him. So he flew a plane to India, travelled by bus to the Himalayas, hired a guide, and hiked for three days to get to this guru. Finally, upon arriving at the guru's humble quarters, he asked the guru for the answer to the ultimate question. The guru, after a couple of moments of silence, said, "When you are hungry, you eat, and when you are tired, you sleep."

This small passage says everything I have been attempting to describe in this entire book, namely, that the key to happiness or being in a state of balance is a matter of detecting that imbalance and knowing how to remedy the situation to bring it back into balance. It really is that simple. However, what gets in the way is our mind.

Stopping the Chatter

Our minds are engaged in constant chatter. Try and stop this chatter, and you will find yourself unable to do so. As I mentioned earlier, stopping the chatter is something that certain spiritual practices teach people to do. It is not something that comes naturally. However, when we get sick, most of the time, we simply need to rest, and the body heals itself with time. When we break a bone, we simply need to set it correctly, and it will grow together on its own. When we cut our finger, we simply have to stop the bleeding and put a Band-Aid on it, and it grows new skin on its own. These processes do not require mind power or for us to do anything in particular. We discovered that our behavior can facilitate or hinder that process, but the process progresses regardless. The mind, in its endless chatter, can actually hinder the healing by creating anxiety, which will burn energy, which is robbed from the body and is no longer available to it to heal itself. The opposite is also true. That is, the mind can actually work to calm the body and give it more energy to heal itself and thus make healing quicker. The idea of stopping the chatter rests on the assumption that the body and the mind are already built to deal with all of the requirements of their biology. All we have to do is stop the internal verbal behavior as well as behavior in general to listen to our body and what it needs. It is only then that the body is able to do what it needs to do. For example, have you ever been so engrossed in an activity that you actually forgot to eat? I once got so focused on computer programming that before I knew it, I looked out the window and the sun was coming up and I hadn't gone to sleep yet. We do this to ourselves frequently. Our internal verbal behaviors keep us not only from experiencing life, but also from doing the things necessary to preserve and nurture our lives.

Now I am not suggesting that all of you reading this book should run out and join some sect that will teach you how to stop the chatter. But there are some simple things that one can do to experience life more fully, or at least without detrimental distractions. I am thinking here of some of my patients who would not be good candidates for such training anyway, and I happen to be much more pragmatic than that. What I aim to illustrate in this section is that our minds, if not properly focused, can get us into trouble. If someone is not happy, they can actually make themselves sick.

In a science news article on happiness, published in August of 2008, it is stated, "Happiness appears to protect against falling ill. One of the mechanisms behind that effect seems to be that chronic unhappiness causes stress, which on its turn reduces immune response" (Erasmus University Rotterdam, "Happiness Lengthens Life," *ScienceDaily*, August 5, 2008).

So the idea here is to behave in ways that make us happy and thereby healthy. The research on happiness is so extensive that you can get lost for hours on the Internet jumping all over the world discussing happiness. And what is happiness? I would argue that happiness is simply a feeling of contentment and of not lacking anything. As we have already discussed, deficit states create an imbalance in the central nervous system, triggering neural, and thus biochemical, events that are experienced as feelings. These feelings can be good or bad experientially, depending on the nature of the imbalance. However, when there is no imbalance, you are not necessarily ecstatic with joy. You are simply feeling OK. You are content, and there is no need to attend to. So the secret to a great life, one that is experienced as pleasant or happy, is to learn to focus on what we need at the present moment and learn how to take care of that need at that moment.

Minimizing the Distractions

Our minds are very susceptible to manipulation. The reason for this, it appears, is that the mind—with its constant internal verbal behavior—is always in a state of readiness to listen, look, and process information, regardless of where or who is providing this stimulation. And as our civilization has evolved around monetary considerations, these monetary concerns have come to dominate our lives so that they are the major stimulus providers in the world as we know it. Thus, most of our thoughts and ideas about what is going on, how we should think and act in relation to those ideas are all dominated by media outlets, whether it is television, radio, or the printed page in the form of magazines, books, and the Internet. Many of those outlets are seemingly free to the public. So who is paying for them? The answer in all cases is the advertisers of the sellers of goods and services. Those sellers of goods and services have a vested interest in making us believe that we need their goods and services. To do this, they have to convince us that we are lacking in some way and that their goods or services will make us whole again. This is the only way they can afford to pay others to provide us with information. Now do you believe that those who are paying for others to provide you with information would allow those providers to give you information that would make any of their products less than good? For example, if ExxonMobil were to be using chemicals in their gasoline that evaporates and causes cancer to all those who come in contact with it and they are sponsoring a news program, do you think that they would allow that news broadcast to expose their crimes? The answer is *no*, I don't think so. So advertisers have a vested interest in lies and misrepresentation, because the goal is not truth; the goal is profits and nothing more.

With the constant drive and encouragement of consumerism presented as the key to your happiness, we are forever distracted and made to feel less than whole because we don't have that car, don't wear that perfume, don't wash with that detergent, etc., ad nauseam. Thus, the media plays a big role in creating disappointment in all of us. One must either accept that all this hoopla is simply meaningless garbage designed to separate us from our money, and move on, or simply limit the exposure one has to those sources of propaganda, such as watching less television or listening to less radio or reading less magazines with lots of glossy photos of products.

One must understand that what is driving the unhappiness movement is largely an artificially created perception that you are not whole without obedience to these constant and relentless messages of what you should do with yourself to be whole. There is a vested interest in the fields of both politics and sales to convince us that we are lacking in some way, and they (those who are telling us we are lacking) are the answer to righting that wrong. This unbridled drive to succeed at any cost has been slowly deteriorating our culture for at least the last fifty years. The only morality is that of profit, and profit produces power, and power is used to buy and control even more propaganda, leading to further misconceptions as to what is truth. So as we started with the quest for truth, we will eventually end with the quest for truth and what keeps us from that truth. The truth can indeed free us, but there are so many distractions that it is difficult to find.

Dealing with Anxiety

I have found that the majority of problems I encounter have their root in anxiety reactions toward the environment that these individuals find themselves in. For example, in the case of a developmentally disabled person, ask yourself how you would feel if your parents placed you in a home where you will be living with five other residents, all of them on the same schedule of when to shower, eat, go to day program, and return from day program, etc., with little, if any, leeway as to what is your particular preference. Imagine that in addition to this scenario, one of the residents exhibits violent temper tantrums on a regular basis, some of which may include assaulting other residents. I am painting a bleak picture on purpose to illustrate some of what my patient population is subjected to. I must add that most of these individuals actually experience a much better life than being at home with their parents, not because they don't have a great time with their parents—they do—but because they are with a peer group that they can relate to more so than their parents and normal siblings. All activities and events are geared toward their functional level and interests. Thus, the picture is not so bad. But it does produce stressful situations for them, at times. The most stressful aspect of such a living environment is the fact that any individual has little control of the entire house. And the simple lack of control is a form of stress that results in anxiety. This anxiety, if not dealt with effectively, can increase and result in inappropriate behaviors. The same can be said within the normal population. If you live in a family of six or seven people, you must learn to accommodate or put up with the others and you can rarely do whatever you want to do. You must do it within the confines of the family structure.

Thus, in implementing training programs for caretakers, parents, or teachers, I try to sensitize them to these internal feelings of the individuals they are caring for that tend to result in behavioral outbursts. To put it simply, anxiety is the feeling of fear, and fear triggers the "fight or flight" response. The organism either becomes aggressive or runs. However, with the developmentally disabled population, where they may not know where to run to, the chances are that they will become aggressive instead. In a behavioral plan, I would suggest giving the anxious client choices and some control over their own schedule. I may ask staff to provide an escape strategy whenever the anxious person is required to go to a crowded and stimulating environment in that an anxious person is easily overwhelmed by too much stimulation. In training, I try to encourage staff to do things that will make the client feel safe. To do so is to adopt an accepting and nurturing attitude. More specifically, reassure the client verbally that everything will be OK. You must convince the client that you are in control and can take care of whatever happens. The trick is *not* to make them feel like you are imposing any control on them. They must be informed that they are free to do whatever they choose and that there are no specific requirements for their participation. However, to discourage self-isolation from occurring with the anxious person, you have to make sure *not* to make lack of participation reinforcing. If the person simply needs a little alone time, allow this as much as possible, but continue to regularly invite them into the activity every few minutes or whenever a new activity starts. In some cases, you have to offer incentives for them to join. This is where rapport is very important. If the rapport is strong, the client is more inclined to want to be with the staff and do what they request of them to do. If there is no rapport, or worse yet, when there is a negative history with the person making the request, the chances of gaining their participation is very unlikely.

The Limitations of Behavior Therapy

Although, as mentioned above, applied behavior analysis is the best option for behavioral problems, there are limitations to that method as it is currently practiced. Behavior intervention alone is sometimes not adequate to stop or manage severe self-injurious behaviors that actually result in injury on a regular basis. The same is true with assaultive individuals who injure others. In both of those cases, psychotropic medications (known as chemical restraints in the laws that regulate such practices with the developmentally disabled) and physical restraints (such as using splints, helmets, gloves or being physically restrained by staff) must be used to protect the individual and those around them. Again, we are faced with behaviors that are largely biochemical in nature and due to, in many cases, neurological damage usually originating in the brain. These biological factors can be somewhat overcome with a combination of medication and behavior intervention. The idea is to calm the individuals to a normal level of functioning, meaning one that is not euphoric or depressed but more like most of us. In that normal state of arousal, the individual is subjected to a behavior intervention plan designed to teach them how to communicate to others or directly meet their needs and preferences, which will be reinforced by staff, if followed. As the behaviors become more automatic and the individual now trusts the environment to meet their needs, a slow titration of psychotropic medications can sometimes be successfully achieved. A word of caution, however, that a fast titration can have significant and long-lasting negative effects that even the reinstatement of previous medications cannot restore. The idea is keep titrating slowly until a slight regression occurs, then return to last previous change in dosage and stay there. Some individuals require a certain amount of psychotropic medications in their system at all times and do not respond well to reductions beyond a certain level. Keep in mind I am still talking about developmentally disabled individuals who, for the most part, were born this way. There are cognitive and physical deficits that may require permanent support. For others, total elimination of psychotropic medications can be successfully achieved. The important thing to remember is that our guide should be the individual in question and *not* some rigid guideline as to when titration should occur. These biological considerations limit the effectiveness of the behavioral approach.

Another example that is problematic in reference to the purely behavioral approach is the case of depression. In most cases, depressed individuals have a reason to be depressed. However, they are operating under a false premise. That premise dictates that they will never find happiness now that this event or point in their life has arrived, so there is no point in trying. Ultimately, the feeling is so hopeless that suicide becomes an attractive option.

The prevailing research indicates that in comparing medication effects, therapy effects, or the effect of both, they consistently find that both offer the best chance at recovery and avoiding suicidal attempts. This is the same as the biological situation mentioned above. But in this case, it is not neurological damage but emotional damage that is driven by faulty cognitions. So we must interfere with these cognitions and change them, thus bringing about a shift in attitude and resulting behavior change. The limitation of the purely behavioristic approach is that it would predict that therapy, which would mostly consist of structured attention to the one exhibiting depression, should increase depression since talking about it and experiencing it brings about attention. What is usually prescribed in a behavioristic approach would be exercise and movement because exercise is incompatible with depression. Yet many have been attended to without exercise and have overcome and left therapy successfully. Because it was more reinforcing knowing that you don't need therapy than the attention that therapy provides. Thus, this would be a case where the behavior is attended to and reinforced with emotional support and verbal mediation, yet it was reduced rather than increased. Anxiety is similar in that the individuals that are anxious would prefer to be alone in a safe area, and attention often increases, and not decreases, the behavior since they become more anxious if they have to answer to someone who is attempting to get them out of the anxiety attack. Such intervention is viewed and responded to as yet another demand made on the system, and behaviors escalate.

In summary, global intervention is providing an atmosphere and lifestyle environment that minimizes the distractions for our consumers, patients, and children by providing opportunities for free time alone, quality time with significant others, activities that are novel and stimulating, training opportunities that promote independence and self-determination, and a supportive environment that engenders a feeling of being loved and accepted by those around them. I find that these quality-of-life issues are much more important to our challenged population than any specific behavioral plan that one can come up with. While I continue to believe in specific behavior plans and provide those to all of my clients that need them, I try to stress to the caretakers that providing a safe and nurturing environment is much more important than simply following a behavioral plan. Thus, I have, in many cases, included quality-of-life reinforcers in my behavior plans so that the individual will be guaranteed at least some of what I am talking about here in their daily lives. This is why I talked about an expanded functional analysis that included such things as the sensory diet that one is on, the rapport between the interventionist and those being treated with that intervention, and the quality of the relationship. A supportive environment is the most important aspect of whether a plan will work or not. Individuals are much more likely to follow your instructions if they feel safe with you. And feeling safe is affected by what the individual thinks and believes. Thus, it is up to us to convince anxious individuals through our words, attitude, and, most of all, behavior that we are there to meet their needs, whatever these needs may be. Setting limits is good, but pushing the person who is anxious is not. In fact, the more we insist on their compliance, the more the anxiety increases. Communicating control of the situation is good, but not controlling the individual who is anxious. Again, we are walking a fine line between making someone feel safe or anxious. This is another example of why I believe that intervention is more an art than a science, because we should guide our actions by how

167

the individual is responding to us, keeping in mind the principle of reciprocity. Thus, we change as we see them change, and we remain flexible as the Taoist text suggests, namely, remaining "soft and pliant as a living tree" and not "hard and brittle as a dead one."

CHAPTER 14

Science and Religion

The Case of Religion

*The tao that can be told
is not the eternal Tao.
The name that can be named
is not the eternal Name.*

*The unnamable is the eternally real.
Naming is the origin
of all particular things.*

This is the first passage of the Tao Te Ching that is assumed to be written by Lao Tzu. I start the chapter with this passage because it appears that the root of most misunderstandings between systems of beliefs has much to do with the particulars of a system and not with the general philosophy of the system. *Tao* in Chinese means "the way." We seem to agree on the general things but not on the specific details. For example, we all want what is best for our children. However, some of us choose to beat them into submission for their own good while others allow them all the freedom they want to express themselves so that they can be the best that they can be and develop a positive self-image. The problem with these characterizations is that they appear to be two diametrically opposed positions but really represent the extremes of the permissiveness gradient. Either position by itself would be lacking because it represents one end of a scale, thus making the gradient off balance. Both positions are part of the same thing. Accepting and rejecting is how we shape behavior. Using only one parameter is inappropriate and can be empirically shown to be inappropriate when dealing with behaviors. The current battle between science and religion, I feel, is just as misguided. The problem is not that we cling to our beliefs, but that we feel compelled to discredit all others as if our own view is the only valid truth and that there can be no other truth. This is the fundamental fallacy of the battle. In actual fact, we are much more alike than different, but our perceptual bent is much more focused on the differences, and we tend to ignore the similarities. Familiarity breeds contempt.

In many ways, this focus on the differences is promoted by many who are positioned to gain from bolstering their position and attract more supporters to their cause. Because more supporters means more money, and more money means more power, and more power means that we can shape the world as we know it to our own benefit at the expense of others. This is because the world is shaped by those in power, and those in power shape the world in their favor. Obtaining that power thus becomes very important for certain groups of people who have been led to believe that this is the *only* way to survive—the "kill or be killed" mentality. This point of view is based on competition and not cooperation. In studying the development of civilizations, we see that we have slowly moved from individual competition of the hunter-gatherer to collective cooperation of the farmer-cultivator. Yet in the past hundred years or so, we are slowly getting back to the competitive lifestyle that is much more intolerant of others rather than cooperative with others. So we seek to increase our group, not for cooperative purposes but for domination purposes—primarily, domination over resources. I am not here passing judgment on which lifestyle is good or bad but, rather, how those lifestyles affect us behaviorally. In a cooperative society, which is what we teach our children in school, getting along with others is the goal. However, as we grow and enter the world of commerce and business, we move into a competitive society whose goal is to beat the opponent and thereby prosper. Thus, one can see the inherent hypocrisy of such a system. We are taught compliance and obedience when growing up, only to find ourselves in a world dominated by competition and a fiercely ruthless marketplace where cooperation is weakness and must be overcome by any means necessary. Also, as we grow, we continue to talk and promote cooperation; but we favor competition whether it is on *American Idol*, the stock market, beating your opponent in sales, beating them in gaining contracts, or beating them in sports. Almost everything in Western culture is based on competition. Cooperation is reserved for small groups whose job it is, again, to beat the competition.

Religions, although most preach cooperation between each other, are collectively competing for memberships in their particular groups and thus have a vested interest in discrediting the others and making the case for their own. The same is true in the attitudes of the applied behavior analysts. They make the case that theirs is the only valid truth and shun consideration of any other forms of therapy or intervention. This narrow view of the world, I would argue, is counterproductive since it does not work in all cases, as mentioned earlier. In my most serious cases, behavior intervention has rarely been enough to stop the damage that some individuals will cause on themselves or others, and the risk of waiting for a behavioral plan to work is simply not a viable option in some cases. In most of these difficult cases, we resort to medications *in addition to* and not *instead of* the behavioral approach.

It is one thing to find a lost sheep and attempt to bring them back into the flock, but it is entirely another thing when you find a happy sheep and then proceed to get them to change to another flock—your own because you are compelled to increase your numbers. This insistence on "you are with us, or against us" is the primary problem here, and all competition makes that mistake—that only one wins and the others lose. As I have attempted to illustrate in the previous chapters, there is no such thing as black and white; we are always operating in a gray area. We are not simply hungry or not. We may not be hungry, a little hungry, or starving; but it is always a matter of degree. It is not an either-or situation where you constantly have to pick one instead of the other. What you pick depends on your need at the time.

We have agreed for the most part, as a people, that everyone has the right to their own religion. Although some countries do not honor this right, they do so for control purposes, and not because they have a better system to offer us. Rather, they seek to impose their system to suppress the people and keep themselves in power.

Nevertheless, religious freedom has been an important issue for just about all civilized cultures ever studied. This belief in the need to respect other people's religions grew out of the suppression in other countries of that freedom and led many of those persecuted to immigrate to this country (USA) to have that freedom. Thus, by implication, we believe that all religions have some validity to them, at least for those who practice those other religions. In practice, too often we are preoccupied with discrediting these other religions that we have vowed to protect and allow their practice. This is yet another hypocrisy in our culture.

The argument is not whether science is right or religion is right. The question is, can these two coexist? Can they be compatible with each other? Are they mutually exclusive?

Every generalized worldview is based on a reality that is valid to the ones practicing it and living by it. And if we attempt to put ourselves in their place, we can actually relate to what they believe in, because many of our beliefs and many of our religious systems are similar concerning the sanctity of life, respecting each other's differences, the need for a moral code of conduct, etc., that is prescribed by each of the religions. Science has its own moral code; it's called the ethics committee. So even in the pursuit of science, it is acknowledged that some sort of morality, duty, or responsibility should be applied to how science will be used and for what purpose. Will it be pursued for its own sake wherever it leads, or should it be directed to benefit the civilization at large? This propensity for finding meaning in everything we do gives rise to these worldviews. Because life, whatever it is, is something given to us, not something we produce ourselves. Even when we have a child through sexual intercourse, the baby grows by the very nature of how the body reacts to certain environmental events, not that we are directing this in any way. While we can have sex on purpose to procreate, there is no guarantee that this act will result in pregnancy. And even when it does, there is no guarantee that it will go to full term. And even if that happens, there is no guarantee that the baby will be intact and free from any disease that could hamper their growth and development. Simply stated, we are not in control.

Applied behavior analysis, which is an empirical science based on verifiable results, is, in many ways, no different than any other religion. The god of that science, applied behavior analysis, consists of empirical results that can be replicated. By implication, one can conclude that this means that if something cannot be proven, verified, and replicated, then it is of no value to the science. Hence, the religion of science views the universe as a set of lawful relationships that can be demonstrated and repeated by anyone. Those things that cannot be demonstrated may be studied, but cannot be considered as viable or real issues, unless first proven to exist. However, science cannot prove that religious beliefs are invalid, and religion cannot prove that science is invalid. But although science rests on empirical facts, where science goes, or the direction in which research is directed, is dependent on subjective parameters. Scientists, in many cases, are working on solving an unmet need. It is the importance of the need that determines the importance of the findings. That need is often a physiological deficit that must be brought back into balance.

The role of religion in human behavior can be seen throughout history. There have been many wars waged in the name of religion. The Crusades is one of the examples in Western cultures, but certainly not the only example known to the world. So whether we believe in the existence of a god or not, and whether we belong to a religion or not, we do have to come to terms with the fact that just about every culture encountered in the natural world has come up with some form of religion that dominates their culture. Thus, religion is a motivating force that we must come to terms with. Understanding the underpinnings of religion and why religions exist would be a useful endeavor for any human being attempting to understand their world. Most civilizations have come to that conclusion that we need to understand, nurture, and respect religion, whatever that religion may be. Having said that, the issue is, why does religion come about in the first place?

As it has been the objective of this entire book to ask why things are the way they are, I am here posing the same question: why is it that religions even occur and flourish? The answer to that, in my view, is that it comes from an internal motivation. Someone is inspired, moved, and driven by their feeling and experience of life that they are moved to share it with others and impress upon them the fact that this other reality exists that is far beyond anything that they have encountered in everyday life.

Usually, it is a transcendent experience that cognitively makes sense, a feeling that everything is all right. As I noted earlier, we are almost never at rest or completely fulfilled. Most of our lives, we are searching for that perfect balance of being without need or want. So an experience of biological as well as cognitive or psychological and emotional balance is quite amazing, since it is rarely experienced. However, many have come close and have reported this experience. Maybe at the sight of your new baby for the first time, the day you actually graduated or passed some very significant step in your life, etc., but rarely is it all of your being feeling completely in tune and content. This unique quality of the religious experience, when communicated to others, tends to find much agreement. There are many who have experienced feelings, whether true or not, of transcendence that others can relate to, even if those other individuals have themselves not had such experiences. Again, whether we believe it or not, it is not really the issue. The issue is that religion *is* a force in human behavior, and a very strong one at that. So that if you can convert someone to your particular religion, you can actually affect and influence their behavior for the rest of their life. This is not a parameter of human motivation to be overlooked or written off or disregarded in any way. It is beyond the matter of whether we believe it. The more important questions are: Do we understand it? Do we know how it works? Is it necessary? Is it unnecessary? Is it good or bad for us? Those are the relevant questions for a topic of human behavior.

Getting caught up in arguments as to whether someone was able to walk on water or part the Red Sea and arguing about the details of a system to discredit and bring down the entire system are really inconclusive exercises in mental gymnastics. Because even if you pick a certain aspect of a system and find fault with it based on your perspective does not necessarily mean that the entire system is incorrect, or even that the part you are interpreting is correctly interpreted. For example, it would be very easy for me to reconcile the various aspects of religious miracles strictly based on the fact that we wish it to be true, or that it would be nice if it was true, or that it is symbolically true. What I am suggesting here is that the mere existence of religion implies that there is a need for such a convention in human cultures. As I have stated from the first chapter of this book to the present chapter, behind every behavior, there is a reason and a force driving it. The functional analysis presumes this by its very construction. We look at the provoking event (the antecedent), the behavior, and the consequence to determine the *function* of the behavior to that individual exhibiting it. Another way to say this is that we find the reason for the behavior by doing the functional analysis. When the functional analysis—the way it has been constructed in modern-day behaviorism—is unable to come to terms with certain aspects of behavior simply because they don't see the provoking event, cannot measure it, and cannot control it, we assume that if our limited senses cannot perceive it directly, then it does not exist. This is absolutely not true and can be proven scientifically beyond the shadow of a doubt in the simple example I gave earlier concerning the light spectrum and what little of that light spectrum we are able to perceive. Bacteria that endanger us and other infectious viruses that can make us sick and even kill us are also things we cannot see without special instruments. By extrapolation, it is ridiculous for any scientific system, especially behaviorism, to actually be so bold as to suggest that the only things that alter behavior are observable and measurable events in the environment. Although it has been proven that those parameters do change behavior, there is no doubt about that; there is doubt about the fact that behaviorism is the whole story.

The greatest examples that illustrate this lack of wholeness are specifically in the area in which behaviorism is the dominant force, namely, in treating developmentally disabled or autistic individuals. Although we are successful in changing behavior, we are rarely successful and are frequently unable to eradicate the inappropriate behaviors altogether. In some cases, as in the revenge case discussed in earlier chapters, sometimes all that is required is a realignment of their thought processes to derive a significant behavioral change. However, a great deal of my work concerns individuals who engage in self-injurious behaviors, or self-stimulatory behaviors that can be injurious, and agitation issues that have been subjected to not only behavioral measures but also psychotropic medications and still persist. I cannot believe that these failures are always due to faulty implementation of behavior plans, as if behaviorism can actually solve all problems. Rather, the failures are due to inherent constraints, as mentioned earlier, on many different levels, whether they be physiological, emotional, or psychological that cannot be overcome completely. It is this aspect of human nature, or behavior in general, that we have to come to terms with. So while we can alter behaviors on many different levels, we do not have complete freedom to achieve anything we want as originally implied by the first person to coin the term *behaviorism*, Dr. Watson. Dr. Watson made the following assertion:

> Give me a dozen healthy infants, well-formed, and my own specified world to bring them up in and I'll guarantee to take any one at random and train him to become any type of specialist I might select—doctor, lawyer, artist, merchant-chief and, yes, even beggar-man and thief, regardless of his talents, penchants, tendencies, abilities, vocations, and race of his ancestors. I am going beyond my facts and I admit it, but so have the advocates of the contrary and they have been doing it for many thousands of years. (*Behaviourism*, 1930, 82)

By his own admission, Watson was going beyond my facts and knew that he could not prove what he was saying. Likewise, I cannot prove every aspect of what I am saying, but the experiential evidence is overwhelming in my favor, as I see it.

We do know that we can significantly impact behavior through the environment. However, when we encounter physiologically challenged individuals who are not normal, meaning they have some kind of physiological anomaly that prevents them from developing as a normal child would, we are able to observe the constraints mentioned above in a much more pronounced fashion. In that case, Watson's assertion does not apply since his assertion rests on a well-formed individual. What that actually means is an open question.

The same can be said about very rich people who, because they have control and resources for their children, attempt to make their children as good as, if not better than, themselves, and often fail. It is actually common that the inheritors of big fortunes tend to squander their opportunities away, unless there are constraints on how to use the money as many have stipulated for this very reason, because they have no motivation to achieve. The epitome of such a scenario is depicted in the movie *Arthur*, where he becomes an alcoholic that is preoccupied with making a spectacle of himself in public until he falls in love, which then gives him the motivation to clean himself up. Again, we come to an unobservable and immeasurable parameter that is life changing. This is something called love. Because of these parameters and these changes in the world that are uncontrollable, it is almost expected that the kind of mentality and psychology to grope with that concept is to assume and imply some greater being or force involved in the process. Again, it is not important whether you believe that this superior or extraterrestrial being or god exists or not. It is enough to know that this influence in the human experience is a relevant behavioral motivator.

When we are talking about science, when we are talking about human behavior, and when we are talking about what causes human behavior, we have to come to terms with the fact that emotional experiences that are provoked by environmental events, primarily other human beings, are very powerful motivators of human behavior; yet they cannot be completely controlled. There are many stories that depict what I am talking about—love stories, tragedies, plays, books, and novels—all of which describe people falling in love when not wishing to do so, or with people that are forced into relationships that should result in love, such as arranged marriages either due to religion, custom, or royalty requirements, yet they do not and eventually part. Remember Princess Diana. These powerful parameters are so prevalent in our culture and so out of our control that we have to come up with a concept to explain them. Because, as noted in many of the previous chapters, control of one's environment is essential for our survival. Thus, when we are confronted with a situation or parameter that we cannot understand and cannot control, we attempt to control it, we label it, we describe it, we worship it, and we try to follow it. This is because we are driven to survive as a result of our genetics, and we are constructed to do so. So from the start, we are not in control; and until the end, we strive to gain control but are not able to fully get a handle on it. We cannot accurately predict what will cause our ultimate death at some point although we know we are going to die. Because regardless of how powerful and empirical behaviorism is, regardless of how effective it is in changing human behavior, it does require the control of all parameters affecting behavior. And when you don't have control of all parameters, you do not have complete control.

It is my contention that this lack of control is precisely why religions are born and flourish, because there is so much in nature that cannot be explained or controlled scientifically, and even those things that can be explained scientifically, much of the time they are beyond our control. So the logic goes like this: if we did not create life, then there must be something beyond us that did because, after all, we are here. In studying nature and science in particular, we find that much of what we see in nature constitutes a lawful set of forces all working together in a nurturing way to sustain the world and our existence in it. So the force that did create life, or at least that made life possible, and constructed the natural world as perfect and as beautiful as it is, must have been and is a much greater and a more intelligent force than any one of its creations. Hence the need for the creation and concept of God. What we attribute to God are all of those things that we cannot explain or account for in simple scientific terms. I would suggest that even if we could explain all aspects of reality in terms of scientific laws and relationships, we still could not account for why these laws work the way they do.

The laws of the universe, whether discovered by science or not, are unalterable. Religions attempt to describe the power behind the creation, while science attempts to describe its rules. Religions recommend we surrender to the power, while science demands that we live by its findings. In both cases, they are describing aspects of the face of God. God appears to be a concept that attempts to label that power that determines human behavior and existence in general. In different parts of the world, that power, God, has been revealed in different ways. In each case, God has been revealed within the culture in its own local terms and by a local person within that culture. But no matter what religion we are talking about, and I include science in this conclusion, the recommendation is always to *surrender* and *accept* the laws of the universe. Accept what *is* in life. Religion is more concerned with the surrender part of the equation, and science is more concerned with the accept part of the equation. The truth for each one of us demands parts from each to fully understand the nature of our being. We have faith, but we look to our objective existence to validate that faith. Thus, my conclusion concerning religion is twofold. The majority of the world has found it to be necessary and relevant to any society, thus making it a legitimate force concerning our behavior; and the level of involvement in it for each of us individually appears to depend on the level of need that we have to adhere to such a practice, which is largely dependent on our reinforcement history and emotional propensity. Meaning that it depends on how well it fits into your life and whether it works for us or not. Which culture and which religion or science we delve into is not as important as how well it works for us. Many argue that we have the freedom to choose, and this deterministic and scientific view of the world does not account for that. But then why surrender? Both spiritual beliefs and scientific dogma demand this acceptance of their particular reality. The whole idea of surrendering is acceptance of that which is beyond our power.

Religion and Freedom

I must here discuss the one major issue between science and religion that seems to separate the two, the issue of freedom. I once had a staff member get visibly angered by my lecture when I started to explain that there is no such thing as freedom. His religious orientation had taught him that we all have a choice, to accept or reject God. And to him, I was one of those who had rejected God. However, I see no difference between religious doctrine demanding my unyielding loyalty to accept all that it has to offer and science demanding that their findings must be accepted since they rest on sound scientific principles. As I mentioned earlier, both demand that we surrender to their system. Whether we do or not largely depends on where we are in our lives and what needs we are experiencing at the time. Everyone has heard of the famous deathbed conversions, murderers finding God in jail, etc., which points to the environmental and situational factors that lead to these conversions to God. I do believe that on the surface, it does appear that we have freedom of choice. However, if you examine human behavior a little closer, you will realize that the choices we make are dependent on our internal state. For example, regardless of what religion you are, you will inevitably get hungry as time passes. And as you get hungry, you will be motivated to eat. The principles discussed earlier apply no matter who you are or what your belief system is. There is no choice in that matter. But you may come back at me and claim, well, yes, it's true that I will get hungry, but I do have a choice of when and what to eat. Again, closer examination will show that your choice will depend on your history and constitution. For example, if you get hungry and you are Jewish or Muslim and what is available are several dishes of pork—such as pork chops, bacon, and ham—with only one chicken option, your choices will be minimized if you are religious and adhere to your faith. Or on the other hand, you are thirsty and what is currently available consists of coffee, milk, and water. If you happen to be lactose intolerant, you are down to only two options. But let's say you never had coffee and don't even like the smell of it. Your choice is then to drink the water, if you can call that a choice. I am not suggesting that we have no say in the matter. What I am saying is that our choices in life have much to do with our constitution, our level of anxiety, our convictions, our religion, and how we were raised. Every experience in life serves to mold us into what we are. Therefore, accepting who we are is the most important aspect of experiencing happiness and freedom. One of my professors once said, "The degree to which you accept your own fate is the degree to which you can experience freedom." What is meant by that is that once we can accept who we are, we are free from living up to other people's expectations, we are free from feeling that we are less than perfect or not as cool or rich or witty as others. If we are or are not any of those things, it is because that is who we are. Not being satisfied with who we are is the root of anxiety. Anxiety burns up energy, which is then not available to your immune system. Your immune system becomes compromised, and you are at risk of infection. And since the world is full of bacteria and germs, you *will* get infected, and your immune system will not be able to help you. Hence, dis-ease leads to disease, as mentioned earlier.

The problems with religions and the various sciences are derived and produced by our thinking brain. To move the science forward, we must accept religion as a legitimate parameter in the causation of behavior; and how one relates to it behaviorally can be and has been subject to manipulation, especially with the help, again, of our thinking brain. Religion goes to the core of our being, as any worldview will. And worldviews, science, and religion all reside in our thinking brain.

Our Thinking Brain

I would argue that most problems in the world are the result of our thinking brain. And wrong thinking results from disturbances in emotional states. And emotional states are temporary human conditions that change all the time. Thus, making decisions based on temporary emotions is very wrong. The reason why this is true is that when we make a decision, we do so for the foreseeable future. So if that decision is based on a temporary emotion, it will soon be invalidated. This is why democracy is a good thing. Because no one person determines what the decision should be, but, rather, the collective makes the decision based on debate, evidence, and the greater good. So if many people are involved, we can be assured that the decision is not based on any temporary emotional state of one person, but rather, it is based on sound judgment of what is best for society at large. Obviously, this process does not always apply since in many periods in history, people have elected leaders based on the emotional mood of the nation at that time. This is done with the help of our cognitive abilities to see the future based on the past and make the best prediction we can as to how that future will be. In these situations, what guides our thinking is our worldview. This is why I started this book talking about the worldview and now return to the worldview.

Our thinking brains are able to predict the future based on the past only because there are lawful relationships in the world we live in. Thus, if we are good observers of how things work, we can extend that vision in the future because lawful relationships do not change from moment to moment; they are constant. However, we have been developing empirical science for hundreds of years; and although we believe in the fruits of science, because we see them all around us, we still have not given up on religion. I would argue that it is precisely the insistence of science to focus on the objective and measurable reality that results in the need for religion. Since science does not speak of or gives us better answers as to how to deal with our emotions, which we are constantly experiencing, many turn to religion for that understanding or system of believing to answer the main question and quest for all of us, which is how to be happy, fulfilled, and not in need. For some, religion has been much more effective in bringing this about, while science, in its insistence on quantifying everything, is too slow and lacking in answers. For others, science is just enough, and they feel no need for religion. Again, which one we pick has little to do with what is right or wrong but has everything to do with what meets our need at the time—our emotional soothing. It is my contention that emotions, although they are varied and sometimes quite complex within the social structure, proceed through a gradient as described earlier with basic needs. Lawful relationships exist between our ability to experience contentment and our ability to deal with arousal levels. As the graphic below attempts to illustrate, arousal levels in any direction divert us away from experiencing contentment. We are genetically programmed to feel better when we move toward the center, and we feel discomfort the farther away we move from the center in any direction. This is why most religions require prayer, contemplation, and silence to bring your focus back to the center.

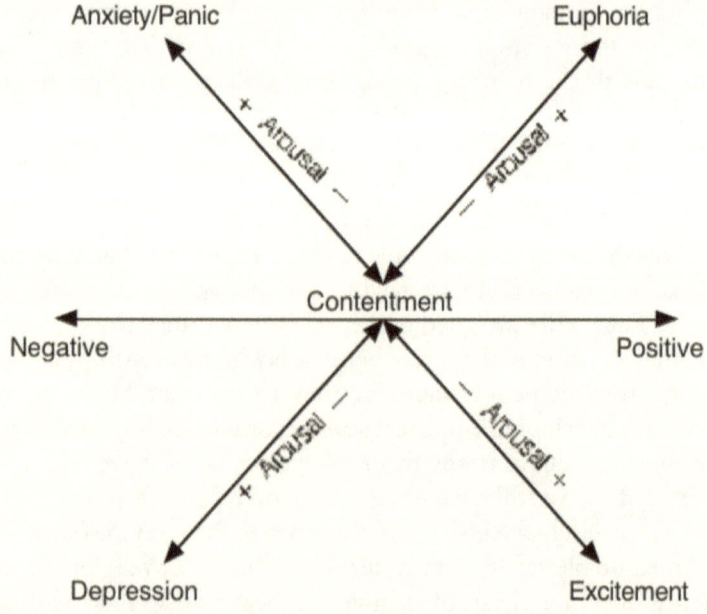

Given the logic of this chapter so far, it should become obvious that where we are in reference to our needs determines *everything*! And using our logic as well as our science, we know that we all have different needs at different times. And although there are systems or worldviews that attempt to answer all of our questions, we don't all ask the same questions and don't all understand and see life the same way. Hence the need for freedom of religion, freedom of thought, etc., that we value in Western democracies. Although we can agree on those principles logically and formulate systems of thought and laws to back them up to create a free society, in actual experience, we do not live by those principles, and our laws are violated every day. Laws are violated not because we don't believe in them but because they do not serve our purpose at the time we are committing that violation. Laws are made to achieve the greatest good for the greatest number in theory. In practice, laws favor those in power and do not favor those that are a threat to that power. Simply consider the laws that allow anyone to buy enough liquor to kill themselves at every street corner, but you can get arrested and do time in jail for possessing marijuana, which has been shown to have therapeutic effects and almost impossible to overdose on and die from as is the case with liquor. I don't want to get political here, but I am simply making the point that those in power will always enforce laws that keep them in power, and oftentimes, there is little morality involved in what is passed and not passed under the guise of what is best for the people. My concern is what is best for each of us in reference to this hypocritical system of what is said and what is done. Too often we see science used to advance power, and objective reality becomes subservient to this power. It is no wonder why people turn to religion, although such abuses of power have been prevalent in that arena as well.

Although our thinking brain can justify anything that is seen, heard, or experienced, it is more accurate to view human behavior from the point of view of its sociobiological frailties. What I mean by this is that given what I have already covered in reference to needs and how they drive behavior through emotional discomfort, the drive for emotional soothing is the prime objective. No one wants to be uncomfortable. And comfort is not always a physiological deficit. However, due to the fact that we are frail biological entities that must survive in a social structure that does not always keep our best interest in mind, we grow anxious. Even when we have all the means necessary to survive—such as a job, a home, and plenty of food to eat—we are still unsettled. Because we know that in a moment's notice, we can have a stroke and become disabled. We could experience an earthquake, and our house may be demolished. We may get raped, robbed, or shot in the bank while making a deposit. Thus, regardless of what we own and the level of protection we supply ourselves with, we remain vulnerable. This is the major problem of having a thinking brain, namely, that the brain is able to imagine a future that may never become reality but that in reality could happen. This is how anxiety is produced. Anxiety is the feeling of impending doom. But as discussed earlier, it is a gradient that spans from totally apathetic to extremely concerned. The extreme ends would be panic on one hand and depression on the other. Thus, when the brain thinks too much about one's own frailty and what could happen in the future, anxiety is increased. When one is immersed into the present, anxiety subsides. Thus, being focused on the present is incompatible with anxiety. Anxiety is based on illusion. The illusion consists of something possibly happening in the future based on the knowledge that it may happen. But the chances of that actually happening are much more remote than the person experiencing them is feeling. Again, anything that brings about this dis-ease will result in depletion of biological energy that could be used to fortify rather than deplete the immune system resources. Hence, dis-ease leads to disease.

Anxiety can be characterized as a bicycle wheel with spokes. When it is revolving at a low intensity, one can still throw things through the spokes of the wheel. In other words, life can still interact with the wheel. However, as the wheel spins faster and faster, the ability for anything to get through diminishes, and what was a permeable surface is now a solid mass that cannot be penetrated. This is why when individuals become extremely anxious, they become immobile. They lose the ability to function and interact with the world. Intervention in those cases necessitates a slowing down of the emotional process through acceptance, reassurance, and a very calm demeanor. Oftentimes, the only thing that will work effectively is medication that attacks this escalation directly.

But just as our thinking brain can bring about feelings of discomfort, the primary benefit of having a thinking brain is that it can also deliver us from this discomfort. If we could convince ourselves that all of these calamities can never happen to us, or that even if they did, it would not be a bad thing, then we could reduce our anxiety related to our mortality. In my view, it is best to simply understand the mechanics of how all of this happens and psychologically surrender to the fact that you are not always in control and that struggling to control that which you can't is a waste of time at the least, and detrimental to your health at the most. Again, religion can serve a role here. If one can believe that there is a God and that God is ultimately in control, then accept whatever happens because of your belief in God who will always do the right thing, then anxiety will be reduced or eliminated. The field of psychosomatic illness has huge databases of research to demonstrate just what I am talking about. I am not suggesting that one should just give up and surrender to whatever happens to them. On the contrary, one can be very active in having the thinking brain serve the physiological well-being through focus on what we know is the truth. This is why it is so important to have a worldview that explains what the truth is to us. Because the truth will free us from wasting our time and energy trying to be fulfilled by something we know not to be adequate to achieve that effect.

The positive aspect of the thinking brain is that it can be shaped, changed, dazzled, or entertained. To make the thinking brain help us in the one area that seems so out of control—our emotions—would be a good thing. And this is what religion provides—an inner peace that everything will work out for the best and there is no need to panic. Like the black guy in the movie *Harold and Kumar Go to White Castle*. When Harry and Kumar found themselves in jail with this black guy, they asked him what he was in for. He explained that they once again mistook him for some other black guy who did something, but he had actually done nothing and was simply minding his own business. So they inquired as to why he was not upset about this. He stated to them that "the universe tends to unfold as it should." And indeed, within minutes, they were all out of jail, and the police was the one having a hard time.

The Problem with Science

The problem with science, as it has evolved in Western cultures, has been its micromanagement of the truth. So each science confines itself to its own little area and attempts to explain the world based on its particular perspective. Sociobiology was an attempt to break out of that mold. Unfortunately, it did not succeed, and the specialties won the battle. I say unfortunately because we as a dominant living specie on the planet are much more complex than any one dimension. Granted, I could describe humans strictly based on chemistry, biology, physiology, psychology, genetics, and behavior. But none of these aspects will describe the whole human experience. Regardless of what we describe and how accurately we can measure it, only each one of us individually can determine whether something feels good or feels bad. And it is mainly those feelings that are the driving force of all behavior. Our minds, our science, and our religions can help to shape our thoughts to put us in a place that feels good all the time. That is the quest. To find truth in any form possible that will reassure us and stop the anxiety, thereby delivering us to contentment.

If one studies religions and philosophical systems, one finds that they have been structured and ritualized as much as any science has. They include beliefs, principles, and behaviors that one must engage in to be whole. But science points their finger at the lack of objective findings of such systems, yet you find them using such systems to guide the direction of their research, and they adhere to their science as the religious person adheres to their religion. Belief systems are belief systems whether they are based on facts or logic. Personally, I prefer a truth that is based on knowledge, logic, *and* experience. In a way, one can view religion as the marriage between cognition and emotion in the realm of experience. Experience is all we get in this life—a certain amount of time to experience being alive. And it is this thing called experience that I now turn to.

CHAPTER 15

Bringing It All Back Home

What We Know So Far

In reviewing what has been presented thus far, one can see
that I've attempted to present the principles and parameters that
influence, control, and shape behavior. Note I did not say human
behavior because the principles of behavior are the same throughout.
These influences fall into two main categories: those that can be
directly observed and those that can be inferred indirectly through
observable behavior. Granted, those things that are inferred are
subject to different interpretation, but what is more important is
what is known to work in real practice. So let us review what those
things are based on the information provided thus far.

We know that everyone wants to be happy. No one wants
to be unhappy. Remembering the electronic self-stimulation
experiments, we know that organisms will hurt themselves just
to feel good. Think of addiction and its role in Western culture.
Thus, *feeling good is one of the primary motivators of behavior.*

We know that being happy depends on being free from
discomfort. Here, discomfort includes emotional and psychological
and physical discomfort, and this is why money cannot buy
happiness, because it cannot effectively deal with emotional and
psychological discomfort. It can only buy you things that will
divert your attention from your unhappiness, but only for a little
while. Again, think of addiction and how we strive to make this
diversion permanent. So the second principle is that *discomfort
motivates and initiates behavior.*

We know that biologically, we will, of necessity, become
uncomfortable concerning different needs at different times and

to varying degrees of intensity. *Experiencing states of imbalance is an inherent part of our nature.*

We know that *learning is guided and shaped by our needs.* Think of ergonomics and how we are essentially lazy about learning things we are not required to know.

We know that *maintaining balance is important in being free from discomfort.* The point of this book—as well as hundreds, if not thousands, of others like it—is doing just that, because it is important and necessary for our survival.

We know that *you can never make a change in the other without making a change in yourself.* Think of the reciprocity principle.

We know that there are *many things that we can see, and many more that we cannot, that influence our behavior.* Emotions are just as valid a parameter as any other visible parameter.

We know that *our minds, or thinking brains, can be our worst disability as well as our greatest savior.* Thinking too much will distract us from experiencing life, and not thinking enough will make us slaves to our emotions.

We know that whatever aspect of behavior we are talking about, that aspect has gradations that go from low to high, and where we are within that spectrum is a fuzzy line. *Opposites are just the same thing viewed from its extreme ends.*

We know that *happiness is a perceptual cognitive view of one's situation.* For example, you could be in a terrible situation, but you celebrate the fact that it is finally happening, the end times are near, and you will soon be with your Savior. If you did not have that belief, you may feel much worse in the same situation.

We know that the *mind or cognitive structure can be altered,* controlled, or focused. We can do this by reading, listening to music, practicing tai chi, or doing drugs.

We know that our entire *life consists of experiences,* some good, some bad; but *all are instructive and shape who we are.*

I will stop now and try to make sense out of these twelve parameters, which I have tried to cover in the previous pages. How they can be used to help bring about this condition or emotional state called happiness is the point of this book. Solving a client's behavioral problem will depend on solving how we can make them feel better about their situation or actually improving their situation. Remember the revenge case, where all that was needed was a cognitive restructuring for behavior change to occur.

First and foremost, the idea and requirement of balance cannot be overlooked or overstated. I would argue that throughout life, one is simply engaged in a balancing act of one's mood, mental state, and behavior in reference to their needs. This is how I see it working. *Mood* is at the top of the pyramid; it is the most important aspect of human existence and behavior, and we all want it. As *mood* changes due to biological, physiological, and psychological need states, the *mind* is employed to determine in what *manner* or behavior the organism needs to engage in to bring about the balance that has been compromised. The most important thing, as mentioned earlier, is to be happy. And to be happy, you must be balanced. To be balanced, you must focus on the relationship between these parameters so that a solution can be found to bring back the balance. But doing so will only be effective for a little while. Because invariably, you will get hungry again, you will get thirsty again, etc., until we perish. Thus, taking care of your temporary imbalance is a constant dance that never ends.

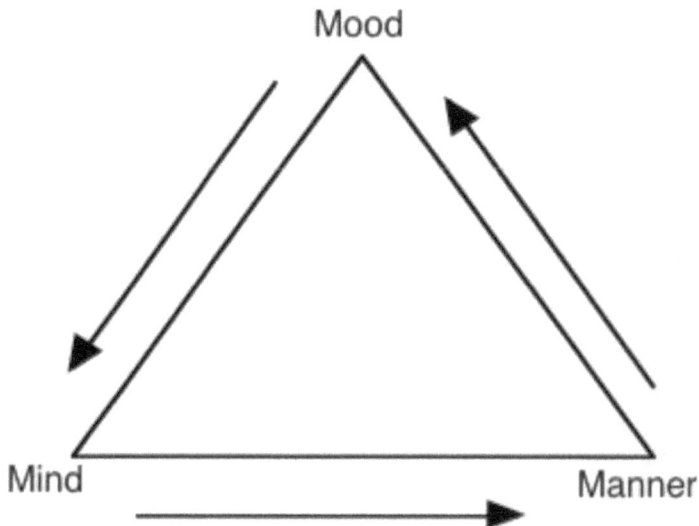

I once had a friend whose significant other died suddenly at an early age. She then told me that her deceased friend had come to her in a dream the night before and revealed to her the secret of life and proceeded to explain to me how this was communicated to her. She said her friend was riding a bicycle and holding on to a transistor radio, something rarely seen these days. But if one is old enough to remember, the biggest problem with those transistor radios was that they were quite sensitive to their position relative to where the signal was coming from. So if you were actually listening to a transistor radio while riding a bicycle, each time you turned a corner or went out of range, you had to readjust the position of the radio for it to continue to play without interference. This deceased friend was telling her that life is really just a matter of aligning yourself appropriately relative to the constant changes that occur in life to continue to listen to the music. Thus, the whole idea was that within the dance that occurs between ourselves and our environment, it is simply a matter of keeping the music playing. Remembering the previous Taoist quote of "remaining pliant and soft," one can see that constant adjustments must be made for one to continue to live in a state of happiness or contentment. Bob Dylan once said in one of his songs, "He who is not busy being born is busy dying." One cannot stand still. That is not one of the options. Thus, we are all caught up in a dance between what we need and what the environment requires of us to alleviate that need. However, in doing so, we must be careful not to interfere with someone else's need, because this will, in turn, affect us.

We Are Our Brothers' Keeper

In applied behavior analysis, the environment is king. All parameters of human behavior can be found there. Although I disagree with this assertion, given my extensive coverage of need states and emotional states, I do believe the environment is extremely important to shaping behavior. Whether we are happy or sad is very much influenced by the environment we find ourselves in. As with the other areas I have covered on applied behavior analysis, I will focus on the aspects of the environment that are usually neglected, mainly the atmosphere and ambience of the immediate environment. Every environment has a tone or feel to it that affects people differently. Thus, although the environment is an objective place that can be described physically, all environments will affect different people differently. Again, the subjective aspects of reality are usually ignored in behaviorism. There are several clients I have whose antecedents for inappropriate behavior consist of loud, noisy, and crowded environments. That is easy enough to address. However, in many other cases, the environmental parameters cannot be fully described because they are largely dependent on the client's mood at the time. For some clients, being in the mall is a nice and pleasant experience. For others, it can provoke a tantrum, but not always. Thus, some individuals are more likely to tantrum in certain places, but it depends on how they are doing at that time.

All environments, as I mentioned earlier with the frequencies at which people operate, have their own frequency at which they operate. If that frequency is incompatible with a particular individual who is there at the time, the chances of a behavioral outburst occurring there is high. The developmentally disabled population is very sensitive to these emotional tones of places. The reason, I believe, is that they are less likely to engage in mental chatter such as what they are going to cook for dinner, how they will pay their bills, etc., thus freeing their minds to focus on the feel of the place rather than on the physicality or meaning of the place. They have a sense of whether they like where they're at or they don't. I have found that developmentally disabled individuals live much more in the now than so-called normal people. If they don't like where they're at, then you will usually observe signs of timidity, resistiveness, or general slowing down. If that particular person has a history of violent tantrums, it would be a good idea to leave the area once you observe those antecedents.

The individual cannot help being affected by their surroundings. This is the aspect of the environment that needs the most attention, namely, how it affects the individual in general. For example, if you go to a nice restaurant with your significant other, expecting to have a nice meal, and a family is seated next to you with a toddler that is unruly, loud, and out of control, your enjoyment of the meal will be compromised, unless of course you like loud, unruly children. At that point, when the environment is interfering with your goal of having a nice meal without loud and unruly children, the important thing is how you interact with the environment. If you get excessively emotional and irate, you may have a bad time even if they remove the offender from the scene since you will be emotionally worked up. If, on the other hand, you take action by asking the waiter to seat you elsewhere where you will not be bothered by the toddler, then you may be able to overcome this obstacle and still have a nice meal. Thus, the *interaction* or *relationship* between you and the environment is paramount for your happiness, as it is with any social situation.

Just as I have described the art of reading behavioral signs in the nonverbal population to understand what they want, one can read the tension, excitement, or apathy of a location. Once you read the situation, if the situation does not suit you, then you must solve this problem by focusing on what you want done and what is possible in that situation. The most important thing is *not* to get excessively emotional and worked up. At the point that you do get emotional is the point where you start inaccurately perceiving the situation. Emotions will fuel whatever feeling you succumb to, and once immersed in it, your ability to effectively deal with the situation is compromised. I teach my staff to *minimize* all reactions to negative behavior and *maximize* reactions to positive behavior so that one is reinforced and the other is discouraged. In the same way, when you encounter a negative situation, you should be minimizing your outrage and maximizing your problem-solving abilities. Getting upset and emotional may solve your problem, but it will be at a price that consists of destroying your inner peace or happiness. Not only that, but you will start upsetting people around you, making them angry and disturbed by your unruly display of emotions. This, in turn, has now infected your environment with much more negativity that could have been avoided had you exercised some self-control that focused on the solution rather than the outrage to push others to come up with a solution for you. Don't sweat the small stuff! Your emotional health is much more important than the stupid things that people may do to upset you.

Getting outraged with others will only pollute your own environment that you are living in and which you are part of. It is for this reason that I conclude that we are indeed our brother's keeper. If we simply get upset and emotionally angry at the stupidity of others, we contaminate our own environment or ambiance. And this cannot be a good thing. We tend to treat negativity with more negativity, and this should be avoided. However, the opposite is also true—that we tend to be more positive around others that are more positive. Thus, attitude is contagious. The point is that environments have a character, just like people, and that character comes to life through the interaction we have with it. The *relationship* we have with an environmental context highly influences how happy or unhappy we feel in that situation. If we are successful in manipulating the environment in such a way as to make it behave in the way we think it should, then we are happy or pleased that things worked out the way we planned them. However, when things don't go our way, we become unbalanced and emotional, as if the environment acted in a strange way and did something we did not expect. This unbalance is experienced as emotion. You feel something and seek to understand the meaning of that feeling so that you can interpret it into behavior. Emotions provoke reactions, and you have to determine what response to engage in before you react. This reaction can be intercepted by our thinking brain to weigh out the risks and benefits of the various possible actions that the individual can make and hopefully choose the one that is most appropriate for the occasion.

The Problem

Life is simply a span of time in which we get to experience ourselves moving through it. If it is true that happiness is the driving force behind every entity in the universe, then finding ways to achieve this perfect balance in our daily lives is in essence finding heaven. Yet it is the nature of the world to always be constantly changing. And if we have to interact with that world, we have to be constantly changing as well, and we are. We are all aging and changing from day to day. However, too often we stick with old ideas even after they have outlived their usefulness because we seek and want security, stability, and predictability in our lives. This need for stability stems from the anxiety I discussed earlier that is the by-product of emotions and fuels the behaviors you will engage in. These are two sides of the same coin: the anxiety necessary to achieve action and the stability that is necessary to achieve rest or contentment.

Putting it in simple terms, we are born, we experience deficits when our biological requirements are not met, we become emotional, we behave and continue to do so until our need has been met, then we get quiet for a while. This cycle repeats itself indefinitely until we expire. The knowledge of this mortality has driven many to invest in objects that outlast the human life span—such as jewelry, buildings, fine furniture, or cars—in an attempt to prolong their existence. Some write books, have children, or start a foundation. But in reality, the only thing that matters as you get closer to death is the quality of your *relationships* with others. If you've been around old people for any length of time, you would know that these nontangible memories of relationships are the only things that really survive within us. It is not the cars, the jewelry, and the objects we accumulate. Only the relationship with our children, our friends, and others who have affected our lives lasts. Yet too often this is the area most neglected in human development. It usually starts right after high school. All your friends scatter to go to universities, take jobs, get married, and have kids. Pretty soon you realize that you've been going along a predetermined program and are simply going through the motions because you don't know what other options there are. Some of us are lucky enough to catch this pattern and interfere with it by making the effort to get together with friends and family and invest in relationships rather than the stock market. Spend time enjoying a meal with the family rather than spending time thinking of ways to make more money.

This type of life I am describing is one that is prescribed by our culture, and although it has relevance, it may have little to do with what's important for you personally. It is a mechanical life—one that meets the requirements of prescribed stereotypes of how things should develop. But true happiness, or balance, is not achieved by following someone else's agenda. Each individual is unique, and it is for this reason that I am inclined to say, "There is no answer!" Due to the fact that we are all different and our need requirements are all different, there can be no prepackaged answer for us. The answer to the big question of how to be totally happy or content is an individual one that only you can answer.

However, if you force my hand to write some method or technique to arrive at an answer, then I shall have to give you general guidelines with a warning that no answer is good all the time, and a broken clock is right twice a day. Things are not what they seem, and telling you there is no answer is, in effect, an answer. So here we go.

The Answer

The answer to life's persistent questions cannot all be covered here. "You can't get there from here," as they say. However, the only answer I will attempt to provide is the one that will point the way to happiness. Whether you are a grown man, a baby girl, or an autistic child, we all want to be happy. We all want to cope effectively with life's challenges. So given all of the above information, how can one utilize these principles to bring about this happiness?

Well, here is how I see it. Since life is simply a series of continuously occurring experiences, the best way to be happy is to be, first and foremost, free from imbalances in your system. This includes biological needs such as appropriate amounts of sleep, eating appropriate amounts of nutrients in your diet, and staying free of infection by practicing good hygiene skills; emotional needs such as getting reinforcement from the social community in which you function, family contact, and time with close friends; and psychological needs of intellectual stimulation, reading books, keeping up on news events, having enough variety in your schedule to avoid boredom. These basic things are the bases of a happy and contented life if they are provided in appropriate amounts, at the right time, and in balance with each other. Note that these basic needs are almost never fully met. No matter how much you eat, you will eventually get hungry, etc., as mentioned earlier. Thus, the answer must be constituted in such a way as not to meet your momentary need only to wait for the next one. No. The answer must be in the form of a general attitude, a certain demeanor about how we approach problems or, more accurately, recurring need states; for these are our primary problems. So what is the best attitude to adopt, and how do you bring this about? I'm glad you asked because I am going to tell you. You adopt an attitude based on logic, rational reasoning, and suitability of who you are.

First of all, you must understand and know that you are not in control of what happens in life. So if you are not in control, this implies that something else is. If that something is beyond your power, and we know it is because we know that we cannot completely control what happens, then we have to accept that we cannot do anything about what has happened. We can only do something in response to what has happened with something we will do in the future. So the first and most important as well as difficult part of adopting an attitude is that you have to accept whatever happens to you as your fate. If that is your fate, then the best attitude to adopt at this point is one of accepting the challenge to deal with this problem, whatever it may be. Knowing that you are a unique human being and that whatever happens to you affects you in a very unique and particular way, you have to view this reality as if the challenge was custom-made for you and only for you to learn from and overcome. Whatever it is, it is something stemming out of your entire history that has brought you to this point, and this point is different from every other point in your life as well as other people's lives. So you can see why I state that there can be no answer. Every challenge is new, every challenge is different, and every challenge we face is something we have to do individually, and absolutely alone. By this, I do not mean that you must face the challenge alone. Only that you are the only one actually engaged in meeting that challenge. The lesson is a unique one for you. And you can recruit any one of your support group that you need to make it through, but it is you that has to make it through, not those that may help you.

So the attitude that one needs to adopt concerning life's challenges is one of acceptance and is characterized as a necessary learning opportunity. And if I can continue to pontificate a while longer about the challenging situation, one must understand and conclude that what happens to you is the result of your entire past and how you have dealt with life thus far, so that you cannot blame others for your misfortune. Because whether you believe in science or religion or both, the world or universe is still a lawful place. Thus, if you were provided with a learning opportunity by environmental circumstances beyond your control, then you must need it, and you would have had to arrive at this juncture sooner or later, and no one can learn this lesson for you. It is for you and you alone. There is something truly positive and unique about these challenges in our lives in that they are all custom-made just for us and largely stem from our shortcomings or deficits. Once we successfully overcome them, that aspect of the self that had a weakness or deficit now has a strength or an asset. How we approach problems and how we approach life has everything to do with whether we are happy or unhappy. Attitude is everything!

Again, I repeat what the Dalai Lama said:

> The basic thing is that everyone wants happiness, no one wants suffering. And happiness mainly comes from our own attitude, rather than from external factors. If your own mental attitude is correct, even if you remain in a hostile atmosphere, you feel happy.

The most compelling argument concerning the brotherhood of man, or women, came from a statement that one of my professors used to say. He posed the question: "When does my breath, which leaves my body and is sucked in yours, stop becoming part of me and start becoming part of you?" Keeping in mind that we are all a connected social structure that must live in this same world of ours, it should be easy to understand and conclude that creating or propagating negative energy in our environment is like polluting our own environment. Even an animal learns not to poop where they eat. In essence, I believe that is exactly what we are doing when we engage in racism, gossip about people, or engage in any negative interaction with others, namely, we are pooping where we will eat. And as mentioned earlier, the opposite is also true. So that if you are very positive in your interactions with others, they will more likely be positive with you. Attitudes are contagious. Research in this area has been quite fruitful in recent years. There was an article in the *New York Times* a few years ago that showed that when a monkey watches a researcher bring an object to his mouth, the same brain neurons fire as when the monkey brings a peanut to its own mouth. In the early 1990s, Italian researchers discovered this phenomenon and named the cells "mirror neurons" (Sandra Blakeslee, *New York Times*, January 10, 2006). This research has been expanded to include humans and how they react when watching each other. Researchers believe that this is the mechanism that mediates empathy. When we do the same experiments with the autistic population, one can see that their lack of empathy is also matched by the lack of mirror cell activity. This would also explain why autistic individuals have a problem with generalizing what they have learned.

The bottom line is that we are all part of an integrated, intertwined social structure that requires our cooperation for us to get our needs met. How we do this depends more on the prevailing social structure rather than on the environment per se. The most obvious example of this is picking out a sexual partner. While the environment can provide us with much opportunity in reference to finding someone suitable for sexual activity, the social rules and rules of engagement will be much more relevant than simply finding someone you would like to have sex with. And what is this social structure? It is a set of rules that determines how one is to interact with others. It is a prescription for a set of behaviors that mediate a relationship. The relationship becomes everything within the social structure. Thus, if we want to be happy, we will have to follow the rules of whatever society we find ourselves in relative to the social structure. Our attitude should be that of accommodation, especially when we want something from the social structure. And being in that structure, we are better off being positive than negative because each will bring about more of the same. Applied behavior analysis, if it can contribute anything significant to the human condition, would be to teach more effective communication skills concerning one's needs and preferences. Because it is these imbalances that interfere with our happiness. You must right the wrong, fill the empty, water the dry, etc. Only then can you be at peace with yourself. And that is true happiness! To achieve this, one has to feel the emotion, then use their cognitive capacities to solve the problem to bring the system back into balance. Thus, the final solution for achieving balance is to utilize our cognitive capacity to solve problems and apply those skills to every challenge that comes our way.

Conclusion

I have attempted to describe an experiential model of behavior that is fluid and in a state of constant adjustment. Based on the above information, I have concluded that behavior is a response to biologically triggered imbalances that attempt to restore the balance the organism had prior to experiencing the emotion of discomfort. This imbalance is usually brought about by known and measurable deficits in the organism that can easily be remedied by replenishing the system with the thing that has been depleted, such as food when hungry and water when thirsty. However, in many cases, the deficit state is not one that is known and, even if known, cannot be measured, observed, or manipulated. I am referring here to emotions of emptiness, not finding purpose for our lives, feeling neglected and insignificant to the big picture, and needing something, but having no clue as to what that something is. These more complex emotions appear to be mysterious and irresolvable but seem to instantaneously disappear once the individual finds what they were missing—usually some other individual that they are able to connect with. They report feeling alive and full of purpose simply because they found a friend. Hence my conclusion earlier that attention, affection, and other emotions are needs that are as pressing, in many ways, as the need for food and water for the organism to survive. For example, these emotional states can be so powerful that they could drastically alter behavior to the point of suicide with no clear antecedent to point to. And even if you can point to relevant antecedents in one case, it would be easy to find many other cases in which those same antecedents were present but which did not result in suicide. So the answer is not quite as clear cut as we would have hoped. The fact of the matter is that due to the structure of our biological existence, we are in constant need of one thing or another. So the answer to life's persistent questions cannot be a specific thing or response to certain stimuli in the environment. The answer is something much more like the development of a style or attitude that we develop concerning how we deal with these constant needs that keep changing from minute to minute. And it is in this area where our minds can be of greatest help, namely, to approach every deficit with the knowledge and understanding that this too shall pass. That emotions are temporary and simply serve the purpose of calling attention to an area you need to nurture. It is not something you want to base decisions on.

The Role of the Mind

Given that we experience deficit states almost constantly that affect and shape our emotional experiences, and given that we must interact with our social environment and physical environments to remedy these deficit states, our primary tool to help guide our behavior to deal with these pressures will be our minds, or cognitive awareness of the parameters of those pressures—the rules by which they operate and what the best methods are in terms of controlling them to make them provide us with what we need. However, as mentioned earlier, our minds are unruly and constantly chattering about one thing or another. I have made the point of discussing the need to stop the chatter and how difficult it is to do that. It almost seems like I am recommending two diametrically opposing attitudes: one that stops the chatter and one that utilizes the chatter to solve problems. But what I am suggesting is that we have to practice control of the chatter, which is the midpoint between stopping the chatter and allowing it to operate without restraint. So instead of being constantly engaged in a stream of thoughts that go from one thing to another, or attempting to stop all chatter, we could allow this chatter to go on unfettered until we begin experiencing discomfort. However, I must point out that if you are too attentive to your thoughts, you may not realize that discomfort is building up. So although you could allow the mind to wander to some degree, you should constantly be checking with your body, making sure you are not uncomfortable in any way. You must be mindful of your emotions, intentions, and constant state of balance or imbalance. Once you detect a discomfort or an imbalance, your cognition should be focused on that. You must attempt to focus your attention on the nature of the discomfort and, once known, behave in such a manner that it will facilitate the resolution of the problem. If you cannot pinpoint the problem, then the best thing to do is something other than what you are doing right now. Obviously, what you are engaged in is not helping you, and you need to try something else. This logical way of dealing with your life is not devoid of emotion. On the contrary, your mind should be directing your behavior and varying your responses until the right emotion is achieved. By this I mean that once the discomfort sets in, you use your mind to solve the problem to bring about a better and more comfortable emotion. In this way, you return to your good mood once your mind has helped to direct you there by engaging in a behavior of a certain manner.

Much of what I have attempted to explain is not that complex. In fact, the problem with science is the fact that in an effort to prove things, they make a very simple process very complex. This is because everything is related to everything else. And as soon as you say it is this thing, then you have to account for how this thing came about and how it is influenced and how it is controlled, etc., until you reach a point of irrelevance. Oftentimes, the problems of our lives are not that difficult. It is us who make it difficult. The answers to life's questions have been answered thousands of times, yet we still publish books like this that attempt to say it a little differently in the hopes that others will understand. This is the nature of existence; nothing stands still, and nothing lasts forever. The one thing we have to perfect is how to go through it and have a good time while we are doing it. The last and final rule I would like to suggest is this: if you are not having a good time doing what you are doing, you need to change how you are doing it, or do something else. This is my general rule with all problems I get called to handle. Whenever we observe a behavioral problem, what is going on at that time is part of the problem. Since we cannot access internal feelings or emotions directly, nor can we ascertain what they are caused by, we cannot use that information to alter behavior. However, we do know that environmental events can indeed alter emotions, and we do have control of some aspects of our environment. Thus, if there is an ongoing problem with a particular individual within that environment, changing the environment will hopefully change the behavior. Actually, it is not quite simple all the time, but it is in some cases, and this is where we start. So the first thing that should be implemented as soon as a behavioral problem occurs is a change in setting, if at all possible. That would be the first layer of the onion, as I mentioned in the introduction. If that does not work, you go deeper, do a functional analysis, and take additional measure. The idea is to do as little as possible and attempt to teach the individual to regain balance on their own rather than doing it for them. Good behavior intervention is intervention that teaches the individual to balance themselves rather than having us do it for them. If they are unable to do so, then teach them to communicate the need for help. If we could all just pay enough attention to our own need states, learn to communicate them, and remedy them, we would all be much happier individuals.

APPENDIX

By Maurice Cayem, PhD, MSPP

INDEPENDENT CONSULTING SERVICES

124 Whispering Oaks Drive, Glendora, CA 91741
(818) 314-0515

REINFORCEMENT SURVEY

A reinforcer is anything that an individual desires, likes, or is willing to work to obtain. Reinforcers can be roughly categorized into four major types:

- Social Reinforcers
- Material Reinforcers
- Activity Reinforcers
- Food & Drink Reinforcers

The type of reinforcer you choose for the individual you are working with will depend on what it is you are trying to accomplish and what are that individual's likes and dislikes. Keep an open mind and experiment with various reinforcers until you find one that is effective enough to achieve the desired result. In using reinforcers keep in mind the following tips:

1) Do not hesitate to change reinforcers in the middle of program if you find that the one you're using has lost its effectiveness.

2) Be sure to include social reinforcers as part of any program you attempt. If the individual requires stronger reinforcers to get started, be sure to give a social reward at the same time you give the stronger reward. This will help to make your social rewards stronger in the long run.

3) Use the most "natural" reinforcer possible. By this, it is meant that you would not want to use a food, drink, or material reinforcer when the individual performs just as well for your praise alone. Likewise, activity rewards

should be used if possible before one goes to the trouble of choosing food, drink, or material reinforcers as part of your program.

4) If you must use food, drink, or material rewards in your program, make an effort to gradually eliminate these rewards and move toward the more "natural" reinforcers of social attention, praise, and fun activities.

With these points in mind, please look at the list below and check the ones that you feel are appropriate and effective enough to use in a behavior program as reinforcers. If none apply, you may fill in your own. The better you know the individual the better you may guess or know what their reinforcers are and the more effective you can be. Please indicate in the list below whether the item in question is liked a lot, a little, or not at all by checking the appropriate box.

I. SOCIAL REWARDS

A Lot A Little Not at all

A. Verbal

	A Lot	A Little	Not at all
1. Being praised about work/performance	[ ]	[ ]	[ ]
2. Smiles	[ ]	[ ]	[ ]
3. Conversation	[ ]	[ ]	[ ]
4. Talking on the phone	[ ]	[ ]	[ ]
5. Receiving phone calls	[ ]	[ ]	[ ]
6. Writing or receiving letters	[ ]	[ ]	[ ]

7. Winks   [ ]   [ ]   [ ]

8. Handshakes   [ ]   [ ]   [ ]

9. Praise in front of others   [ ]   [ ]   [ ]

10. Other _____ [ ]   [ ]   [ ]

11. Other _____ [ ]   [ ]   [ ]

A Lot A Little Not at all

B. Physical

1. Hugging   [ ]   [ ]   [ ]

2. Horsing around   [ ]   [ ]   [ ]

3. Kissing   [ ]   [ ]   [ ]

4. Pats on shoulder, head   [ ]   [ ]   [ ]

5. Strocking/massaging   [ ]   [ ]   [ ]

6. Tickling   [ ]   [ ]   [ ]

7. Spinning   [ ]   [ ]   [ ]

8. Holding hand/Holding on lap [ ]   [ ]   [ ]

9. Patty-cake   [ ]   [ ]   [ ]

10. Other _____ [ ]   [ ]   [ ]

11. Other _____ [ ]   [ ]   [ ]

II. ACTIVITY REWARDS

	A Lot	A Little	Not at all
1. Choosing a family outing	[ ]	[ ]	[ ]
2. Playing sports (football, baseball, etc.)	[ ]	[ ]	[ ]
3. Skiing	[ ]	[ ]	[ ]
4. Bicycle riding	[ ]	[ ]	[ ]
5. Watching TV	[ ]	[ ]	[ ]

	A Lot	A Little	Not at all
6. Coloring	[ ]	[ ]	[ ]
7. Riding horses	[ ]	[ ]	[ ]
8. Visiting the library	[ ]	[ ]	[ ]
9. Getting haircuts	[ ]	[ ]	[ ]
10. Reading	[ ]	[ ]	[ ]
11. Camping	[ ]	[ ]	[ ]
12. Gardening	[ ]	[ ]	[ ]
13. Cooking meals	[ ]	[ ]	[ ]
14. Playing table games	[ ]	[ ]	[ ]
15. Writing letters	[ ]	[ ]	[ ]

16. Helping with cleaning chores   [ ]   [ ]   [ ]

17. Playing pool   [ ]   [ ]   [ ]

18. Playing with animals   [ ]   [ ]   [ ]

19. Fishing   [ ]   [ ]   [ ]

20. Eating at restaurants   [ ]   [ ]   [ ]

21. Going to the movies   [ ]   [ ]   [ ]

22. Using the telephone   [ ]   [ ]   [ ]

23. Painting   [ ]   [ ]   [ ]

24. Hunting   [ ]   [ ]   [ ]

25. Swimming   [ ]   [ ]   [ ]

A Lot A Little Not at all

26. Wrestling   [ ]   [ ]   [ ]

27. Playing on the trampoline   [ ]   [ ]   [ ]

28. Singing   [ ]   [ ]   [ ]

29. Dancing   [ ]   [ ]   [ ]

30. Flying a kite   [ ]   [ ]   [ ]

31. Playing catch   [ ]   [ ]   [ ]

32. Going to church   [ ]   [ ]   [ ]

33. Sewing   [ ]   [ ]   [ ]

34. Outings   [ ]   [ ]   [ ]

35. Car rides   [ ]   [ ]   [ ]

36. Listening to self on tape recorder [ ]   [ ]   [ ]

37. Other _____ [ ]   [ ]   [ ]

37. Other _____ [ ]   [ ]   [ ]

III. MATERIAL REWARDS

A Lot A Little Not at all

A. Nonmonetary

	A Lot	A Little	Not at all
1. Toys	[ ]	[ ]	[ ]
2. Books/Comics	[ ]	[ ]	[ ]
3. Magazines	[ ]	[ ]	[ ]

A Lot A Little Not at all

	A Lot	A Little	Not at all
4. Stamps/Coins	[ ]	[ ]	[ ]
5. Models (airplanes, etc.)	[ ]	[ ]	[ ]
6. Records	[ ]	[ ]	[ ]
7. Grooming aids	[ ]	[ ]	[ ]
8. Radio	[ ]	[ ]	[ ]
9. Gold stars on charts	[ ]	[ ]	[ ]
10. Games	[ ]	[ ]	[ ]
11. Tools	[ ]	[ ]	[ ]

	A Lot	A Little	Not at all
12. Arts and crafts	[ ]	[ ]	[ ]
13. Puppets	[ ]	[ ]	[ ]
14. Certificates	[ ]	[ ]	[ ]
15. Sports items	[ ]	[ ]	[ ]
16. Play-Doh	[ ]	[ ]	[ ]
17. Soap bubbles	[ ]	[ ]	[ ]
18. Balloons	[ ]	[ ]	[ ]
19. Pet the dog	[ ]	[ ]	[ ]
20. Water gun	[ ]	[ ]	[ ]
21. Jewelry	[ ]	[ ]	[ ]
22. Bicycle	[ ]	[ ]	[ ]
23. Pen/pencil/crayons	[ ]	[ ]	[ ]

A Lot A Little Not at all

	A Lot	A Little	Not at all
24. Baseball cards	[ ]	[ ]	[ ]
25. Clothes	[ ]	[ ]	[ ]
26. Playing cards	[ ]	[ ]	[ ]
27. Dolls/stuffed animals	[ ]	[ ]	[ ]
28. Puzzles	[ ]	[ ]	[ ]
29. Other _____	[ ]	[ ]	[ ]
30. Other _____	[ ]	[ ]	[ ]

B. Monetary

1. Money   [ ]   [ ]   [ ]

2. Checking account   [ ]   [ ]   [ ]

3. Savings account   [ ]   [ ]   [ ]

4. Play money   [ ]   [ ]   [ ]

IV. FOOD & DRINKS

	A Lot	A Little	Not at all

A. Food

	A Lot	A Little	Not at all
1. Cookies	[ ]	[ ]	[ ]
2. Candy	[ ]	[ ]	[ ]
3. Cereal	[ ]	[ ]	[ ]
	A Lot	A Little	Not at all
4. Cake/donuts/pie	[ ]	[ ]	[ ]
5. Popcorn	[ ]	[ ]	[ ]
6. Cracker Jacks	[ ]	[ ]	[ ]
7. Potato chips	[ ]	[ ]	[ ]
8. Pretzels	[ ]	[ ]	[ ]
9. Cheetos	[ ]	[ ]	[ ]
10. Peanut butter	[ ]	[ ]	[ ]

	A Lot	A Little	Not at all
11. Marshmallows	[ ]	[ ]	[ ]
12. Meat	[ ]	[ ]	[ ]
13. Cheese	[ ]	[ ]	[ ]
14. Ice cream/sherbert	[ ]	[ ]	[ ]
15. Nuts	[ ]	[ ]	[ ]
16. Cotton candy	[ ]	[ ]	[ ]
17. Baby food	[ ]	[ ]	[ ]
18. Fruit	[ ]	[ ]	[ ]
19. Pickles	[ ]	[ ]	[ ]
20. Hamburger	[ ]	[ ]	[ ]
21. French fries	[ ]	[ ]	[ ]
22. Pizza	[ ]	[ ]	[ ]

	A Lot	A Little	Not at all
23. Raisins	[ ]	[ ]	[ ]
24. Jell-O/pudding	[ ]	[ ]	[ ]
25. Chewing gum	[ ]	[ ]	[ ]

B. Drinks

	A Lot	A Little	Not at all
1. Apple juice	[ ]	[ ]	[ ]
2. Cranberry juice	[ ]	[ ]	[ ]

3. Water   [ ]   [ ]   [ ]

4. Milk   [ ]   [ ]   [ ]

5. Milk shake   [ ]   [ ]   [ ]

6. Sodas _____   [ ]   [ ]   [ ]

7. Grape juice   [ ]   [ ]   [ ]

8. Cocoa   [ ]   [ ]   [ ]

9. Orange juice   [ ]   [ ]   [ ]

10. Gatorade   [ ]   [ ]   [ ]

11. Tea   [ ]   [ ]   [ ]

12. Coffee   [ ]   [ ]   [ ]

A Lot A Little Not at all

13. Lemonade   [ ]   [ ]   [ ]

14. Kool-Aid   [ ]   [ ]   [ ]

15. Other _____ [ ]   [ ]   [ ]

16. Other _____ [ ]   [ ]   [ ]

_____   _____

Name   **Date**

Learning Modalities Assessment

Prior to implementation of any formal training interventions, staff should evaluate the individual's learning style by doing a learning modalities assessment. This consists of asking five basic questions:

1. In what setting does the individual prefer to work?

   a. Alone

   b. With someone else

   c. With a small group

   d. As part of a large group

2. In what places does the individual work best?

   a. Quiet   h. Open

   b. Active   I. Standing

   c. Bright   J. Kneeling

   d. Dim   k. Sitting

   e. Warm   l. Laying down

   f. Cool   m. Moving around

   g. Structured

3. What type of reinforcers does this individual enjoy?

   a. Special privileges

   b. Praise when finished

   c. Self-satisfaction

   d. Getting recognition from others

   e. Getting praised while they are working

4. The individual will work at an activity for as long as?

   a. 5 minutes at a time

   b. 20 minutes at a time

   c. 1 hour at a time

   d. More than 1 hour at a time

   e. He or she finishes what they said they would do

   f. He or she finishes what another asked them to

5. When does the individual perform best?

   a. In the morning

   b. In the afternoon

   c. In the evening

   d. Before eating

   e. After eating

Behavioral Contract

Name: _____   Date: _____

I, _____, agree to enter into this contract
whereby I will earn a lunch outing with _____,
to any restaurant I want and order any lunch I would like to have
 provided I do not assault anyone for one month.

Should I assault anyone within that month period will result in not
earning that outing and the contract will be renewed so that the clock
begin again starting with the first day after the last assaultive episode.

_____   _____
Client Signature   Interventionist Signature

BIBLIOGRAPHY

Alhazen, (1011-1021). *Book of Optics*. Retrieved January 23, 2009 from *http://www.statemaster.com/encyclopedia/Book-of-Optics*

In text (Alhazen, 1011-1021)

Bacon,F (1620). *The new organon: Or true directions concerning the interpretation of nature*. Retrieved July 31, 2009 from *http://www.constitution.org/bacon/nov_org.htm*

In text (Bacon, 1620)

Blakeslee, S. (2006, January 10). Cells that read minds. *The New York Times*, Retrieved October 15th 2008 from *http://sandrablakeslee.com/articles/mirror_neurons_jan06.php*

In text (Blakeslee, 2006)

Bowlby,J, Ainsworth, M (1992). The origins of attachment theory: John Bowlby and Mary Ainsworth Inge Bretherton. *Developmental Psychology 28,759-775.*

In text (Bowlby & Ainsworth, 1992)

Bozarth, M.A. (1994). Pleasure systems in the brain. 5-14. Retrieved November 24, 2008 from *http://wings.buffalo.edu/aru/ARUreport01.htm*

In text (Bozarth, 1994)

Castaneda, C. (1971). *A separate reality: Further conversations with Don Juan*. Simon & Schuster, New York, New York.

In text (Castaneda, 1971)

Cayem, M (1986). Compliance training using caretakers as co-therapists in the severely and profoundly retarded as a method for decreasing maladaptive behaviors. *University microfilms international.* Ann Arbor Michigan.

In text (Cayem, 1986)

Darwin,C (1872). *The expression of emotions in man and animals.* Oxford University Press, Oxford.

In text (Darwin, 1872)

Harlow, H (1958). The nature of love. *American Psychologist 13, 673-685.*

In text (Harlow, 1958)

Joe Namath. (2009, September 15). Brainy Quote. Retrieved September 15, 2009, from *http://www.brainyquote.com/quotes/authors/j/joe_namath.html*

In text: (Namath, 2009)

Lundin, R.W. (1979). *Theories and systems of psychology.* Lexington, Massachusetts: D.C. Heath and Company.

In text (Lundin, 1979)

Olds, J., & Milner, P. (1954). Positive reinforcement produced by electrical stimulation of the septal area and other regions of rat brain. *Journal of Comparative and Physiological Psychology, 47,* 419–427.

In text: (Olds, Milner, 1954)

Pribram, K.H. (1971). *Languages of the brain: Experimental paradoxes and principles in neuropsychology.* Englewood Cliffs, New Jersey: Prentice Hall Inc.

In text (Pribram, 1971)

Rincover, A (1981). Some directions for analysis and intervention in developmental disabilities: An editorial. *Analysis and intervention in developmental disabilities.* 2,109-115.

In text (Rincover, 1981)

Russo,D.C, Cataldo, M.F., & Cushing,J.P. (1981). Compliance training and behavioral co-variation in treatment of multiple behavior problems, *Journal of Applied Behavior Analysis, 14, 209-222*

In text (Russo et. al. 1981)

Schachter,S.& Singer,J.E.(1962).Cognitive,Social,and Physiological Determinants of Emotional State. Psychological Review, 69(5), 379-399. Retrieved February 11, 2009, from *http://www.psychwiki.com/wiki/The_Schachter-Singer_Theory_of_Emotion*

In text (Schachter & Singer, 1962)

Science Daily (2008, August 5). Science Daily: your source for the latest research news. Retrieved January 23, 2009 from *http://www.sciencedaily.com/releases/2008/08/080805075614.htm*

In text (Science Daily, 2008)

Siegel, D. J. (2007). *The mindful brain: Reflection and attunement in the cultivation of well-being.* W.W. Norton & Company, Inc. New York, New York.

In text (Siegel, 2007)

Skinner, B.F. (1992). *Verbal Behavior.* Acton, Massachusetts: Copley Publishing Group.

In text: (Skinner, 1992)

Tsu, L. (1997). Tao Te Ching, Vintage Books, USA

In text (Tsu, 1997)

Watson, J.B. (1913). Psychology as the behaviorist views it. 20, 158-177. Retrieved October 15, 2008, from *http://psychclassics. yorku.ca/Watson/views.htm*

In text (Watson, 1913)

Watson, J.B. (1919). *Psychology: From the standpoint of a behaviorist.* J.B. Lippincott, Philadelphia, Pennsylvania.

In text (Watson, 1919)

Watson, J. B. (1930). Behaviorism (Rev. ed.). New York: Norton.

In text (1930)

Whitney, C, Britt, A (1907 April—September). *The OUTING Magazine.* Volume L, 749.

In text (Whitney & Britt, 1907)

Wilson (1975). *Sociobiology: The new synthesis.* Cambridge, Massachusetts: The Belknap Press of Harvard University Press.

In text (Wilson, 1975)

www.ingramcontent.com/pod-product-compliance
Lightning Source LLC
Chambersburg PA
CBHW061359280526
45784CB00001B/308